Merry Christmas From Tennessee

by

Betty Jane McClanahan

McClanahan
Publishing House

Cover design and book layout by James Asher Graphics

Manufactured in the United States of America

All book order correspondence should be addressed to:

McClanahan Publishing House, Inc.
P. O. Box 100
Kuttawa, KY 42055

1-800-544-6959

www.kybooks.com
books@kybooks.com

This book is dedicated to all who have eaten my cooking blunders and continued to encourage me.

Merry Christmas from Tennessee

is my gift to you and yours to enjoy
throughout the holiday season. The recipes I have included are easy to
prepare and a pleasure to share with those you love. My hope is that you
will enjoy using this cookbook in celebrating this wonderful time of year.

Merry Christmas to you!

Table of Contents

Appetizers

Office Party Crab Ball

One 8-ounce package cream cheese
1 pound fresh or canned crabmeat
One 10 or 12-ounce bottle seafood sauce
Horseradish to taste

Soften cream cheese; mix with crab; roll into a ball. Refrigerate until ready
to serve, then add horseradish to sauce, if desired, and pour sauce over the
ball. Serve with crackers. Covers 30 to 50 crackers.

Christmas Caviar

Two 8-ounce packages cream cheese
1 Tablespoon chopped parsley
1 teaspoon basil
¼ teaspoon lemon juice
One 2-ounce jar red caviar
1 bunch scallions, chopped

Soften cream cheese; add parsley, basil and lemon juice. Form into a ball
and cover with the caviar just before serving. Place chopped scallions
around sides of ball and serve with crackers.

Holiday Evening Crab Puffs

1 cup water
1 stick margarine
¼ teaspoon salt
1 cup flour
4 eggs
One 6-ounce can crabmeat, drained and flaked
½ cup shredded sharp Cheddar cheese
3 green onions, chopped
1 teaspoon Worcestershire sauce
1 teaspoon dry mustard

In a medium saucepan combine water, margarine and salt. Bring to a boil; reduce heat to low; add flour and stir until mixture leaves sides of pan and makes a ball. Remove from heat; add eggs one at a time, beating with a wooden spoon until well blended and smooth. Add the crabmeat, cheese, onions, Worcestershire sauce and dry mustard, stirring until blended. Drop by heaping teaspoons onto an ungreased baking sheet. Bake at 350 degrees for 25 minutes. Makes 50 puffs.

Crab Cakes with Lime

⅔ cup mayonnaise
1 Tablespoon lime juice
¼ teaspoon ground red pepper
Two 6-ounce cans crabmeat, drained and flaked
1 cup dry bread crumbs, divided
1 small jar pimentos, chopped and drained
2 Tablespoons minced green onions
2 Tablespoons butter

Mix mayonnaise, lime juice, red pepper, crabmeat, ½ of the bread crumbs, pimentos and green onions. Form into 8 patties; roll in remaining bread crumbs. Cook patties in butter about 3 minutes on each side.

Sauce

½ cup mayonnaise
½ cup sour cream
1 Tablespoon lime juice

Combine ingredients. Serve sauce on the side.

Cranberry Nut Cups

One 3-ounce package cream cheese, softened
½ cup butter, softened
1 cup flour
1 egg
¼ cup brown sugar
1 teaspoon vanilla
⅓ cup finely-chopped fresh or frozen cranberries
4 Tablespoons chopped pecans

Combine cream cheese, butter and flour; cover and chill for 1 hour. Pinch off small portions of chilled dough and place in small muffin tins to form piecrusts. In mixing bowl mix egg, sugar and vanilla. Stir in cranberries and pecans. Spoon into muffin tins. Bake at 325 degrees for 30 minutes; cool in the pan. Makes 24 cups.

Little Oyster Pies

½ cup butter
6 ounces cream cheese
¾ cup flour
1 Tablespoon cold water
3 small cans smoked oysters, drained

Cut butter and softened cream cheese into flour; add water; chill. Using a portion of the chilled dough at a time, roll on well-floured board to ⅛-inch thick; cut 36 rounds with a biscuit cutter. Place smoked oysters on half of each round; fold over and seal edges with fork, prick top. May freeze. Bake at 450 degrees for 20 to 30 minutes. Makes 36 appetizers.

Perfect Pickled Shrimp

1½ pounds cooked fresh or thawed frozen medium-size shrimp
2 small onions, sliced
6 bay leaves
¾ cup vegetable oil
½ cup celery leaves
¼ cup pickling spice
1 Tablespoon salt
¼ cup white vinegar
3 Tablespoons capers
2 teaspoons celery seeds
1 teaspoon salt
3 to 4 drops hot sauce

Combine shrimp, onions and bay leaves in zip-top plastic bag. Combine remaining ingredients in a jar. Close and shake. Pour over shrimp. Seal bag and refrigerate 24 hours, turning occasionally. Discard bay leaves. Drain shrimp and display on a plate covered with lettuce leaves. Makes 6 to 8 appetizer servings.

Shrimp Dip

One 8-ounce package cream cheese, softened
1 small package Roquefort cheese
1 Tablespoon mayonnaise
1 to 3 Tablespoons milk
Finely-chopped celery
Chopped parsley
Garlic salt
½ teaspoon Worcestershire sauce
One 8-ounce package small frozen cooked shrimp, thawed

Combine all ingredients, adding shrimp last. Cover and refrigerate several hours before serving. Serve with crackers or chips. Makes about 2 cups of dip.

Water Chestnut Pick-ups

1 package onion dip mix
¼ cup milk
One 3-ounce package cream cheese, softened
¼ cup chopped green pepper
¼ cup chopped pimento
¼ cup chopped almonds
½ cup chopped cooked chicken
One 8-ounce can sliced water chestnuts, drained

Combine onion dip mix, milk and cream cheese; add green pepper, pimento, almonds and cooked chicken. Place a teaspoon of mixture on a slice of water chestnut and place another slice on top. Makes 25 pick-ups.

Warm Spinach Balls

One 10-ounce box chopped frozen spinach, cooked and well drained
1 cup herb bread stuffing mix
1 onion, finely chopped
3 eggs, slightly beaten
⅓ cup melted butter
¼ cup grated Parmesan cheese
1 Tablespoon garlic powder or garlic salt

Mix all ingredients. Form balls using 1 teaspoon of mixture for each. Bake on a lightly-greased baking sheet for 20 minutes at 350 degrees.

Antipasto Kabobs

One 9-ounce package refrigerated cheese-filled tortellini
One 14-ounce can quartered artichoke hearts, well drained
One 6-ounce jar pitted ripe olives, well drained
½ pound 2-inch-round thin-sliced pepperoni
One 8-ounce bottle reduced-fat Parmesan Italian salad dressing

Cook tortellini according to package directions; drain and cool. Thread tortellini and next 3 ingredients on 25 six-inch wooden skewers. Place over a large baking dish; drizzle with salad dressing. Cover and chill for 4 to 5 hours; drain before serving. Makes 25 skewers and serves 12.

Antipasto Dip

One 14-ounce can artichoke hearts, drained and chopped
Two 4-ounce cans sliced mushrooms, drained and chopped
One 4-ounce jar diced pimentos, drained
1 cup pimento-stuffed olives, chopped
½ cup chopped green pepper
½ cup chopped celery
½ cup vegetable oil
½ cup finely-chopped onion
1 clove garlic, minced
⅔ cup white vinegar
2 teaspoons Italian seasoning
1 teaspoon seasoning salt
1 teaspoon sugar
½ teaspoon pepper

Combine first 6 ingredients. Heat oil over medium heat; sauté onion and garlic; add vinegar and remaining ingredients; bring to a boil; pour over combined vegetables; cover and refrigerate overnight. Drain and serve on crackers.

Tomatoes Rockefeller

1 carton cherry tomatoes
One 10-ounce package frozen chopped spinach, thawed
½ cup chopped onion
1 garlic clove, minced
¼ cup butter
½ cup soft bread crumbs
1 teaspoon salt
1 teaspoon chopped thyme
½ cup freshly-grated Parmesan cheese
2 large eggs, lightly beaten

Cut tops off tomatoes, scoop out pulp and turn tomatoes upside down to drain. Drain spinach; press between paper towels. Sauté onion and garlic in the butter. Stir in spinach, bread crumbs and remaining ingredients; cook stirring constantly until eggs are set. Spoon mixture into tomato shells and place in a lightly-greased 11x17-inch baking dish. Bake at 350 degrees for 12 to 15 minutes. Makes 30 appetizers.

Cheese Cake Appetizers

Three 8-ounce packages cream cheese, softened and divided
3 Tablespoons chopped pimento-stuffed green olives
2 teaspoons olive juice
1 Tablespoon mayonnaise
1 cup shredded sharp Cheddar cheese
One 2-ounce jar diced pimento, drained
1 teaspoon grated onion
¼ cup butter, softened
2 cloves garlic, pressed
1 teaspoon Italian seasoning

First Layer: Beat 1 package cream cheese at medium speed with an electric mixer; add olives and olive juice. Spread mixture into bottom of a plastic wrap-lined 8x4-inch loaf pan. Second Layer: Beat 1 package cream cheese at medium speed until creamy; add mayonnaise and Cheddar cheese. Stir in pimento and onion. Spread over first layer. Third Layer: Beat remaining package of cream cheese at medium speed; add garlic and Italian seasoning. Spread garlic mixture over pimento mixture. Cover and chill 4 to 6 hours until firm. Present with assorted crackers and/or fresh fruit. Serves 8.

Holiday Ham Appetizers

3 cups biscuit mix
1½ cups finely-chopped cooked ham
4 cups shredded Cheddar cheese
½ cup Parmesan cheese
2 Tablespoons chopped parsley
2 teaspoons spicy mustard
⅔ cup milk

Mix all ingredients; shape into 1-inch balls. Place 2 inches apart on a lightly-greased jellyroll pan. Bake 20 to 25 minutes in a preheated 350-degree oven. Serve warm. Makes 7 dozen.

Red and Green Nachos

1 pound hot pepper Monterey Jack cheese, shredded
¼ pound Cheddar cheese, shredded
One 16-ounce bag round tortilla chips
1 small jar red jalapeño jelly
1 small jar green jalapeño jelly

Blend cheeses; spread over chips; decorate with the red and green jellies; slip under broiler and broil until bubbly. Serve hot.

'Tis the Season Bacon Rounds

One 8-ounce can refrigerated crescent rolls
One 3-ounce package cream cheese, softened
5 slices bacon, cooked and crumbled
3 Tablespoons finely-chopped onion
1 teaspoon milk
Grated Parmesan cheese

Unroll crescent rolls and separate into 4 rectangles; press perforations to seal.
Combine cream cheese and next 3 ingredients; spread on rectangles. Roll
up, starting at long side and press together edges to seal. Cut each roll into
8 slices; place on ungreased baking sheet. Sprinkle with Parmesan cheese.
Bake at 375 degrees for 12 to 15 minutes. Serve warm. Makes 24 to 30.

Yummy Rumaki

One 16-ounce carton chicken livers
1 cup soy sauce
1 cup brown sugar
½ teaspoon paprika
One 8½-ounce can whole water chestnuts, drained
½ pound bacon

Marinate livers in mixture of soy sauce, brown sugar and paprika overnight in the refrigerator. Drain livers. Roll a liver around each water chestnut and wrap ⅓ to ½ slice of uncooked bacon around the liver fastening it with a toothpick. Bake at 400 degrees for 20 minutes, turning once. Broil for a few seconds to make bacon crisp. Serve warm.

No Fuss Swedish Meatballs

1 pound sausage
⅓ cup fine dry bread crumbs
1 egg, beaten
½ teaspoon sage
1 Tablespoon vinegar
1 Tablespoon soy sauce
2 Tablespoons brown sugar
½ cup ketchup

Mix first 4 ingredients; shape into balls and brown in skillet. Combine remaining ingredients and pour over meatballs; cover and simmer 30 minutes; serve hot using toothpicks. Makes approximately 40 per pound of meat.

Garlic-Cheese Ball

Two 3-ounce packages cream cheese
1 Tablespoon mayonnaise
1 Tablespoon Worcestershire sauce
1 clove garlic, pressed
1 teaspoon dry mustard
2 to 3 dashes hot sauce
4 cups shredded, sharp Cheddar cheese
2 teaspoons paprika
1 teaspoon chili powder

Combine first 6 ingredients in a large bowl; beat at medium speed of electric mixer until creamy. Add Cheddar cheese; form into 2 balls. Combine paprika and chili powder. Roll balls in mixture. Cover and chill at least 8 hours. Serve with crackers. Makes 2 cheese balls.

Beverages

Tipsy Eggnog Punch

1 quart coffee-flavored ice cream
2 quarts commercial eggnog
3 cups cold coffee
2 cups whiskey
1 pint whipping cream, whipped
Nutmeg

Combine all ingredients except nutmeg in a punch bowl; stir until blended; sprinkle with nutmeg. Serves 15.

Poinsettia Punch

2 quarts cranberry juice, chilled
1 quart vanilla ice cream, softened
One 10-ounce package frozen sliced strawberries
1½ cups sugar
1 teaspoon vanilla
2 cups whipping cream, whipped
One 2-liter bottle ginger ale, chilled

Combine first 5 ingredients; fold in whipped cream; add ginger ale. Serve in punch cups or large glasses. Serves 32 punch cups or 16 large glasses.

Prancer's Champagne Punch

Two 10-ounce packages frozen raspberries in syrup, thawed
½ cup lemon juice
½ cup sugar
One 750-ml bottle red rosé wine, chilled
1 quart raspberry sherbet
One 750-ml bottle Asti Spumante or champagne, chilled

In blender, puree raspberries. In a large punch bowl, combine raspberries, lemon juice, sugar and wine; stir until sugar is dissolved. Just before serving scoop sherbet into punch bowl and pour Asti Spumante over; stir gently. If desired, garnish each glass with a mint leaf and raspberry. Serves 10 to 15, depending on size of cups or champagne glasses.

Dessert Brandy Cream

2 pints vanilla ice cream, softened
½ cup brandy
⅓ cup crème de cacao
¼ cup hazelnut liqueur
¼ teaspoon nutmeg
Whipping cream, whipped

In blender, process first 4 ingredients until smooth; pour into 4 large glasses.
Serve with whipping cream on top sprinkled with nutmeg. Serves 4.

Christmas Eve Irish Coffee

½ cup milk
¼ cup Irish whiskey
1 quart coffee flavor ice cream
1 teaspoon instant coffee
One 10-ounce container frozen whipped topping, thawed

In blender, blend ingredients until smooth. Serves 4.

Special Occasion Iced Tea

1 cup lemonade mix
½ cup instant tea mix
½ cup sugar
3 cups white grape juice
15 cups water

Stir until all has dissolved. Serve over ice. Makes 1 gallon.

Cooked Eggnog

6 eggs
¾ cup sugar
2 cups milk
1 cup brandy
¼ cup rum
1 Tablespoon vanilla
2 cups whipping cream, whipped

Combine eggs and sugar in saucepan; add milk. Cook over medium heat stirring continuously for 18 to 20 minutes, until mixture thickens and coats a metal spoon.   Remove from heat; add remaining ingredients. Serves 8.

Hot Spiced Cranberry Tea

3 cups boiling water
½ cup sweetened lemon-flavored ice tea mix
3 cups cranberry juice cocktail
Lemon slices
Whole cloves
Cinnamon sticks

Heat together water, tea mix and cranberry juice cocktail. Pour into mugs; place a slice of lemon with cloves in each mug and stir with a cinnamon stick. Makes 6 cups.

Beside the Fire Coffee Punch

1½ squares semi-sweet chocolate
1 cup water
½ cup sugar
¼ cup instant coffee
⅛ teaspoon salt
1 quart milk
1 cup whipping cream, whipped

Combine first 5 ingredients; heat until blended; add milk, but do not boil. Serve hot with whipped cream. May use unsweetened chocolate if you don't want it too sweet.

Under the Mistletoe Wassail

4 cups hot tea
4 cups cranberry juice
4 cups apple juice
3 cinnamon sticks
6 cloves
1 cup sugar
2 cups orange juice
¾ cup lemon juice
1 orange, sliced
1 lemon, sliced

Combine ingredients in a slow cooker or large pan. Simmer for at least 1 hour. Remove orange and lemon slices after about 1 hour so that they do not make it bitter. Makes 12 to 16 cups.

Eggnog by the Spoonful

4 eggs, separated
½ cup sugar
Pinch of salt
1 to 2 Tablespoons rum flavoring
2 cups whipping cream, whipped

Beat egg yolks, sugar and salt until thick and lemon-colored. Stir in rum flavoring; fold mixture into whipped cream. Beat egg whites until stiff; fold gently into egg-cream mixture; chill thoroughly. Serve in glass cups with spoons. Serves 12.

Breads

Good Morning Cranberry Scones

2½ cups flour
½ cup sugar
2 teaspoons baking powder
½ teaspoon orange peel
½ cup butter
2 cups Cranberry Almond Crunch cereal, lightly crushed, divided
1 egg
One 8-ounce container vanilla yogurt
3 Tablespoons orange juice
2 Tablespoons brown sugar
1 Tablespoon butter, melted

Mix flour, sugar, baking powder and orange peel; cut in butter until mixture resembles coarse crumbs. Stir in 1½ cups of cereal. Beat egg; stir in yogurt and orange juice; add to flour mixture; stir until soft dough forms. With hands floured, shape into a 9-inch round; place on a greased baking sheet. Score into 12 wedges. Mix remaining cereal, brown sugar and 1 tablespoon melted butter; sprinkle over dough. Bake at 425 degrees for 10 to 12 minutes. Makes 12 scones.

Nutty Cranberry Muffins

2 cups flour
3 teaspoons baking powder
1 cup sugar
½ teaspoon salt
½ cup orange juice
½ cup milk
⅓ cup butter, melted
1 egg, slightly beaten
1½ cups fresh or frozen cranberries
½ cup chopped pecans
2 Tablespoons grated orange peel

Combine flour, baking powder, sugar and salt. In separate bowl combine orange juice, milk, butter and egg; stir into dry ingredients; fold in cranberries, pecans and orange peel. Fill greased or paper-lined muffin tins three-fourths full. Bake at 400 degrees for 18 to 20 minutes. Makes 12 muffins.

Christmas Eggnog Muffins

3 cups flour
½ cup sugar
3 teaspoons baking powder
¼ teaspoon salt
½ teaspoon nutmeg
1 egg
1¾ cups commercial eggnog
½ cup vegetable oil
½ cup golden raisins
½ cup chopped pecans

In a large bowl combine flour, sugar, baking powder, salt and nutmeg. In separate bowl, combine egg, eggnog and oil; stir into dry ingredients. Fold in raisins and pecans. Fill greased or paper-lined muffin tins two-thirds full. Bake at 350 degrees for 20 to 25 minutes. Makes 15 muffins.

Puffy Popovers

1 cup flour
½ teaspoon salt
1 cup milk
2 eggs

Beat all ingredients with whisk until smooth. Fill well-greased deep muffin tins three-fourths full. Bake 40 to 45 minutes at 425 degrees. Makes 5 to 9 popovers.

Christmas Morning Angel Biscuits

5 cups self-rising flour
1 teaspoon soda
⅓ cup sugar
1 cup solid shortening
2 cups buttermilk
2 packages dry yeast, dissolved in ¼ cup warm water

Combine dry ingredients. Cut in shortening; add buttermilk and yeast mixture. Mix well; roll out dough and cut. Place biscuits on cookie sheet and freeze. Place in plastic bags after freezing. Bake frozen at 400 degrees for 10 to 15 minutes. Easy and very good.

Easy Cranberry Bread with Apricot Butter

1 package cranberry bread mix
½ cup chopped, dried apricots
1 teaspoon grated orange peel
1 cup water
1 egg

Combine ingredients; stir well. Bake in greased and floured 9x5-inch loaf pan at 350 degrees for 50 minutes. Serve with Apricot Butter.

Apricot Butter

½ cup butter, melted
¼ cup apricot preserves

Beat together until light and fluffy.

Gingerbread

1 cup butter
1 cup sugar
2 eggs
1 cup dark corn syrup
2½ cups flour
½ teaspoon salt
1½ teaspoons ginger
1 teaspoon baking soda
1 cup boiling water
Whipped cream

Blend butter and sugar; add eggs; add corn syrup and mix thoroughly. Sift together the flour, salt and ginger; fold into the butter mixture. Dissolve baking soda in boiling water. Add to butter mixture. Bake in a greased 9x13-inch baking dish at 350 degrees for 30 to 40 minutes. Serve with whipped cream. Serves 12.

Biscuits with Garlic

5 cups biscuit mix
1 cup shredded Cheddar cheese
One 14½-ounce can chicken broth with roasted garlic

Mix ingredients to form a soft dough. Drop by spoonfuls onto ungreased baking sheets. Bake at 350 degrees for 15 to 20 minutes until browned. Makes 24 biscuits.

Greek Cornbread

1 stick butter
1 small box corn muffin mix
One 10-ounce box frozen chopped broccoli, drained
4 eggs
8 ounces cottage cheese
8 ounces sour cream

Melt butter in skillet in oven. Combine the remaining ingredients in a bowl. Pour melted butter into batter; pour batter into the skillet. Bake at 350 degrees for 30 to 45 minutes. Good with White Chili.

Company's Coming Dinner Rolls

1 cup milk
¼ cup sugar
1 teaspoon salt
¼ cup butter
2 packages dry yeast
½ cup warm water
2 eggs, beaten
5¼ cups flour
Melted butter

Bring milk to almost boiling but do not boil; add sugar, salt and butter. Cool. Soften yeast in warm water; add milk mixture, eggs and 2 cups flour; beat until smooth; add enough additional flour to form a soft dough. Knead for 8 to 10 minutes. Place in a greased bowl, turning to grease top. Cover and let rise about 30 minutes until doubled in size. Turn onto a lightly-floured board; shape into crescents; cover and let rise in warm place until double in size, at least 30 minutes. Brush with melted butter. Bake at 400 degrees 10 to 15 minutes. Makes 3 dozen rolls.

Light Cornbread

1 cup milk
6 Tablespoons sugar
2 teaspoons salt
½ cup butter
½ cup warm water
2 packages dry yeast
2 eggs, beaten
3½ cups flour
1¾ cups yellow cornmeal

Combine milk, sugar, salt and butter; heat until milk is scalded and butter is melted. Combine warm water and yeast; stir until dissolved. Add milk mixture, eggs, flour and cornmeal; beat until well mixed. Spoon batter into 2 well-greased loaf pans. Cover and let rise until double in bulk, about 1 hour. Bake at 375 degrees for 30 minutes. Makes 2 loaves.

Simply Easy Spoonbread with Corn

One 8½-ounce package corn muffin mix
One 8-ounce can cream-style corn
One 8-ounce can whole kernel corn, drained
One 8-ounce container sour cream
½ cup butter, melted
2 large eggs

Stir together all ingredients; pour into a greased 9x5-inch loaf pan. Bake at 350 degrees for 35 minute.

Sourdough Bread

One ¼-ounce package dry yeast
3½ cups warm water, divided
7 cups flour, divided
¼ cup nonfat dry milk powder
2 Tablespoons butter, melted
2 Tablespoons sugar
1 teaspoon salt
Cornmeal

Using a 4-quart glass bowl, dissolve yeast in 2 cups warm water; let stand for 5 minutes. Stir in 2 cups flour until smooth. Cover loosely with a towel and let stand in warm place (80-90 degrees) to ferment for 48 hours; stir several times daily. The mixture will become bubbly and rise, have a "yeasty" sour aroma and a transparent yellow liquid will form on the top. Stir in milk powder, butter, sugar, salt and remaining water and enough remaining flour to form a soft dough. Do NOT knead. Cover and let rise in a warm place until doubled, about 1½ hours. Turn onto a floured surface; punch dough down. Do NOT knead. Divide in half. Shape each into a round loaf. Heavily grease baking sheets and sprinkle with cornmeal. Place dough on prepared pans. Cover and let rise until doubled, about 30 minutes. With a sharp knife, make three diagonal slashes across top of each loaf. Bake at 350 degrees for 10 minutes. Brush loaves with cold water; bake 35 to 40 minutes longer until golden brown. Yields 2 loaves, or may be shaped into 24 rolls instead of loaves. Bake 10 minutes, then 20 to 25 minutes after brushing with water.

Grandmother's Dill Bread

1 package active dry yeast
¼ cup warm water
2 Tablespoons sugar, divided
One 8-ounce carton cream-style cottage cheese
1 Tablespoon minced dried onion
2 Tablespoons butter
2½ teaspoons dried dill seed, divided
1 teaspoon salt
¼ teaspoon baking soda
1 egg, beaten
2 to 2½ cups flour

In small bowl combine yeast, water and 1 Tablespoon sugar. In medium saucepan, combine cottage cheese, 1 Tablespoon sugar, dried onion, 1 Tablespoon butter, 2 teaspoons dried dill seed, salt and baking soda. Heat until butter melts. In large bowl combine dissolved yeast mixture, cottage cheese mixture and egg. Using a wooden spoon stir in as much of the flour as possible. Turn dough onto a lightly-floured surface. Knead in enough of the remaining flour to make a moderately soft dough, 3 to 5 minutes. Shape dough into a ball. Place in a lightly-greased bowl, turning once to grease surface of dough. Cover and let rise in a warm place for about 1 hour or until doubled in size.

Punch dough down. Turn out onto a lightly-floured surface. Shape by patting or rolling it into a 7-inch round loaf. Place dough in a greased loaf

pan. Cover and let rise in warm place until double in size, about 30 to 40 minutes. Brush dough with 1 teaspoon of melted butter and sprinkle with the ½ teaspoon dill seed. Bake at 350 degrees for 40 to 45 minutes. Remove from pan immediately. Makes one large 16-serving loaf.

Seasoned Flat Bread

One 10-ounce package refrigerator pizza dough
¼ cup olive oil, divided
1 large onion
2 teaspoons minced garlic
1½ teaspoons Italian seasoning
¼ teaspoon salt
¼ teaspoon pepper
¾ cup Parmesan cheese

Unroll pizza dough, place on a baking sheet; using wooden spoon handle make indentations in dough about 1 inch apart. Brush with 2 tablespoons olive oil. Bake at 425 degrees for 10 to 12 minutes. Cut onion into thin half slices. Sauté onion in remaining 2 tablespoons of olive oil on medium heat until tender; add garlic and next 3 ingredients; sauté 1 minute. Place onion mixture on top of bread and sprinkle with cheese. Bake at 425 degrees for 5 minutes until cheese is melted. Serves 4 to 6.

Cranberry Nut Bread

2 cups flour
1 cup sugar
1½ teaspoons baking powder
½ teaspoon baking soda
½ teaspoon salt
¼ cup butter
1 egg, beaten
1 Tablespoon grated orange rind
¾ cup orange juice
¾ cup chopped nuts
1 cup chopped cranberries

Combine dry ingredients; cut in butter. In a separate bowl blend together egg, orange rind and orange juice. Add to dry ingredients. Mix well. Add nuts and cranberries. Bake in a greased 9x5-inch loaf pan at 350 degrees for 35 to 45 minutes. May be frozen.

Breakfast
&
Brunch

Christmas Holidays Breakfast Pizza

One 8-ounce can refrigerated crescent dinner rolls
6 eggs, beaten
½ pound bacon, cooked and crumbled
1 cup shredded Cheddar cheese
½ cup sliced fresh mushrooms

Spread rolls into lightly-greased 12-inch pizza pan, pressing firmly to seal perforations. Set this in a 375-degree oven for about 2 minutes to set the crust, so it is not too soggy. Combine eggs, bacon, cheese and mushrooms; pour over crust. Bake at 375 degrees for 12 to 15 minutes.

Burritos for Breakfast

1 cup hash brown potato mix with onions
2 cups hot water
Six 8-inch flour tortillas
6 eggs, well beaten
½ pound pork sausage, cooked and crumbled
Dash of salt
Pepper to taste
2 Tablespoons butter
¾ cup shredded Cheddar cheese
Picante sauce
Ripe olives, sliced
Sour cream
Guacamole

Combine potato mix and water; stir and let stand covered about 15 minutes; drain. Wrap tortillas securely in foil, heat at 350 degrees for 10 minutes. Combine hash browns, eggs, sausage, salt and pepper. Cook egg mixture in butter until done, but not overdone. Place ½ cup eggs on tortillas, sprinkle with shredded cheese, roll up, placing seam-side down. Serve with sour cream, ripe olives, guacamole and picante sauce. Serves 6.

French Toast for the Family

1 cup packed light brown sugar
½ cup butter
2 Tablespoons light corn syrup
Two 6¼-ounce packages frozen butter crescent rolls, thawed
6 eggs
1½ cups milk
1 teaspoon vanilla
¼ teaspoon salt

Stir together first 3 ingredients in saucepan. Cook over low heat, stirring often, until butter melts. Pour into a lightly-greased 9x13-inch baking dish. Place crescent rolls in a single layer over syrup. Whisk together eggs and next 3 ingredients; pour over rolls. Chill at least 8 hours. Remove from refrigerator and let stand at room temperature 30 minutes. Bake at 350 degrees for 45 minutes. Serves 6.

Crunchy French Toast

3 eggs
1 cup half & half
2 Tablespoons sugar
1 teaspoon vanilla
¼ teaspoon salt
8 slices French bread
1 cup crushed corn flakes
Strawberry syrup
Fresh strawberries
Whipping cream, whipped

Combine eggs, half & half, sugar, vanilla and salt. Dip bread in egg mixture, then in crushed corn flakes. Place in greased 15x10-inch baking dish. Cover with foil and freeze 2 hours or more. Bake at 425 degrees for 15 to 20 minutes, turning once. Serve with syrup, strawberries and whipped cream.

Country Ham with Redeye Gravy

1 pound center-cut country ham slices ·

Cook covered over low heat in a large cast-iron skillet about 30 minutes until tender. Pass Redeye Gravy. Serves 6 to 8.

Redeye Gravy

2 cups hot strong coffee
¼ cup brown sugar

Mix coffee with brown sugar. Pour into ham drippings in the skillet; bring to boil, stirring to loosen any ham particles left in skillet. Cook on medium heat for about 10 minutes. Makes about 1 cup gravy.

Mountain Top Brunch Eggs

1 pound fresh mushrooms, sliced
¼ cup melted butter
3 Tablespoons flour
2 cups whipping cream
1 egg yolk
1 teaspoon beef bouillon granules
2 Tablespoons finely-grated onion
2 Tablespoons parsley
¼ teaspoon salt
¼ teaspoon pepper
8 eggs
Grated Parmesan cheese
4 English muffin halves, toasted

Sauté mushrooms in butter about 5 minutes; remove with slotted spoon and set aside. Add flour to butter; stir until smooth; cook 1 minute. Gradually add mixture of whipping cream, egg yolk, bouillon granules and onion, stirring until mixture is thickened. Stir in mushrooms, parsley and seasonings. Pour into a lightly-greased 9x13-inch pan. Press mushroom mixture to make 8 compact indentures. Break an egg into each. Sprinkle with Parmesan cheese. Bake at 350 degrees for 7 to 8 minutes until eggs are done. Serve over English muffin halves. Serves 8.

Eggs Benedict

Butter
2 English muffins, split
4 slices Canadian bacon, cooked
4 poached eggs

Butter muffins, place slice of Canadian bacon on each muffin, then poached egg and top with Hollandaise Sauce.

Hollandaise Sauce

3 egg yolks
Salt and pepper
2 Tablespoons lemon juice
½ cup butter

In top of double boiler beat egg yolks, salt and pepper; gradually add lemon juice, stirring constantly. Add one-third of the butter to egg mixture; cook over hot but not boiling water until butter melts. Add another third of the butter, stirring constantly; as sauce thickens, stir in remaining butter. Cook until thickened. Makes ¾ cup. Serves 2.

Margaret's Creamy Grits

8 cups half & half
1 teaspoon salt
½ teaspoon garlic powder
½ teaspoon pepper
2 cups quick-cooking grits
One 8-ounce package cream cheese, cubed
One 12-ounce package shredded Cheddar cheese
1 teaspoon hot sauce

Bring first 4 ingredients to a boil; stir in grits; return to boil; cover and reduce heat. Simmer 5 minutes, stirring occasionally. Add cream cheese and the remaining ingredients. Stir until cheese melts. Serves 8 to 12.

Quiche for a Brunch

¼ pound ham, chopped
1 cup shredded Monterey Jack cheese
1 cup chopped cooked chicken
1 unbaked pie shell
4 eggs
2 teaspoons Dijon mustard
1 cup milk
Salt and pepper to taste

Place ham, cheese, and chicken in pie shell. Beat eggs, add, mustard, milk and salt and pepper. Pour over ingredients in pie shell. Bake 45 minutes at 350 degrees. Serves 6.

Country Christmas Crab Benedicts

1 pound fresh crabmeat, drained and flaked
¼ cup butter, melted
½ teaspoon salt
¼ teaspoon pepper
6 English muffins, split and toasted
12 eggs, poached

Sauté crabmeat in butter for about 5 minutes; add salt and pepper. Spoon small amount of crabmeat on each English muffin half; top with a poached egg and cover with Brandy Sauce.

Brandy Sauce

¼ cup butter
3 Tablespoons flour
1½ cups milk
¼ teaspoon salt
2 Tablespoons brandy
Hot sauce to taste

Melt butter in saucepan; add flour, stirring until blended. Gradually add milk; cook until thickened. Stir in brandy and hot sauce. Serves 6.

Soups
&
Salads

Dinner Party Artichoke Soup

1 small onion, finely chopped
4 Tablespoons butter
2 Tablespoons flour
½ cup milk
One 14-ounce can artichokes, drained and chopped, reserving liquid
3 cups chicken consommé or chicken bouillon
3 egg yolks
½ cup cream
1 teaspoon lemon juice
Salt to taste

Sauté onion in butter. Blend in flour and milk, stirring until well blended. Add artichoke liquid and consommé; bring to a boil. Combine egg yolks and cream. Remove 1 cup of hot liquid and add to egg yolk mixture; stir well and return to saucepan. Add chopped artichokes, lemon juice and salt. May garnish with a spoonful of sour cream and/or lemon slice. Serves 6 to 8 depending on serving bowl.

Tortilla Soup

½ cup chopped onion
1 Tablespoon cooking oil
2 cooked chicken breasts, chopped
4 tomatoes chopped
1 clove garlic, minced
One 10-ounce package 6-inch corn tortillas, cut into thin strips and divided
One 14½-ounce can chicken broth
One 14½-ounce can beef broth
2 Tablespoons tomato sauce
¼ teaspoon cumin
½ Tablespoon chili powder
1 bay leaf
¼ teaspoon salt
¼ teaspoon ground red pepper
½ cup shredded Colby-Monterey Jack cheese blend
½ avocado, peeled and sliced

In large heavy pan, sauté onion in cooking oil, add the remaining ingredients except cheese and avocado. Cook 20 minutes or longer. Serve topped with cheese and a slice of avocado. Serves 6.

Neighbor's Soup

1¼ cup chopped onion
¼ cup butter
¼ cup flour
½ teaspoon minced garlic
⅛ teaspoon hot sauce
4 cups milk
1 cup shredded sharp Cheddar cheese
½ cup chopped cooked ham
½ cup chopped cooked turkey
Crumbled bacon
Chopped tomato
Chopped parsley

Sauté onion in butter in Dutch oven on medium heat; add flour, garlic and hot sauce; stir 1 minute. Gradually stir in milk; cook until thickened and bubbly. Reduce heat; add cheese, ham and turkey. Blend until heated, being careful not to let it boil. Serve topped with bacon, tomato and parsley. Serves 5.

A great way to use Christmas dinner leftovers.

Aunt Evelyn's Chicken Noodle Soup

1 large onion, chopped
1 Tablespoon butter
3 cups chopped chicken
Three 14-ounce cans chicken broth
1 can cream of mushroom soup
1 can cream of chicken soup
One 8-ounce package noodles
1 cup chopped celery
1 cup chopped carrots
1 teaspoon poultry seasoning
1 teaspoon pepper
2 cups milk
Shredded Cheddar or Swiss cheese

Sauté onion in butter; add remaining ingredients except cheese. Bring to boil; reduce heat and simmer 45 minutes. Top with cheese. Serves 6.

Jingling Jambalaya

1 large onion, diced
1 large bell pepper, diced
1 pound smoked sausage, cut into ¼-inch slices
1 Tablespoon olive oil
4 cups chopped, cooked chicken
3 cups uncooked long grain rice
2 cans French onion soup
One 14½-ounce can chicken broth
One 14½-ounce can beef broth
2 to 3 teaspoons Creole seasoning
2 to 3 teaspoons hot sauce

Sauté first 3 ingredients in oil; add chicken and remaining ingredients. Bake covered at 350 degrees for 40 minutes, stirring after 30 minutes. Serves 4.

Seafood Chowder

2 medium potatoes, diced
1 large onion, diced
1 pint oysters, drained
¼ cup butter
2 Tablespoons flour
1 teaspoon salt
½ teaspoon pepper
1 Tablespoon Worcestershire sauce
Hot sauce to taste
Two 8-ounce cans minced clams, drained
One 16-ounce package frozen small shrimp, thawed
1 quart milk, scalded
Chopped parsley

Boil potatoes and onion until done; drain. Sauté oysters in butter 2 or 3 minutes. In large saucepan combine flour, salt, pepper, Worcestershire sauce and hot sauce; blend until smooth; add potatoes, onion and remaining ingredients except parsley. Heat on low for 20-30 minutes. Serve with parsley sprinkled on top. Serves 10.

Wild Rice Florentine Soup

2 cups chopped celery
2 cups chopped carrots
2 cups chopped onions
3 sticks butter, divided
8 cups chicken broth
2½ cups cooked wild rice
2 Tablespoons thyme
2 bay leaves
1 teaspoon salt
1 teaspoon pepper
1 cup flour
Two 10-ounce boxes frozen spinach
1 pint half & half

Sauté vegetables in 1 stick butter; add chicken broth, rice and seasonings. Melt 2 sticks butter in saucepan; add flour and stir until smooth; add to soup, stirring constantly until thickened. Add spinach and half & half; heat thoroughly and serve. Serves 6 to 8.

Cream of Broccoli Soup

Two 10-ounce packages frozen broccoli
¼ cup chopped onion
4 Tablespoons butter
5 Tablespoons flour
3 cups chicken stock
1 to 2 cups half & half
¼ teaspoon salt
¼ teaspoon pepper

Cook broccoli according to package directions. Drain well and cut into small portions. Sauté onion in butter, add flour, stirring until blended. Gradually add chicken stock, stirring until smooth; add broccoli and remaining seasonings. Use the half & half to obtain desired consistency. May garnish with croutons, parsley, and/or paprika. Serves 6.

French Onion Soup

4 cups thinly-sliced onions
½ stick butter
2 Tablespoons flour
½ teaspoon sugar
Four 10½-ounce cans beef broth
½ cup dry vermouth or dry white wine, optional
5 to 6 slices French bread, sliced 1-inch thick
2 Tablespoons grated Parmesan cheese
¼ cup Gruyere or Swiss cheese

Sauté onions in butter; add flour and sugar, stirring until blended. Slowly add beef broth. Simmer 30 minutes. Add vermouth. Toast French bread, sprinkle with Parmesan cheese. Place soup in bowls, cover with French bread, top with cheese, slip under broiler until cheese melts. Serve immediately. Serves 6.

Merry Mushroom Soup

2 Tablespoons butter
3 Tablespoons flour
⅛ teaspoon dry mustard
½ teaspoon salt
Cayenne pepper to taste
4 cups chicken bouillon
1 pound fresh mushrooms, sliced
⅓ cup dry sherry
½ cup cream, scalded
½ pint whipping cream, whipped
Chopped almonds

Melt butter; add flour, mustard, salt and cayenne. Gradually stir in chicken bouillon and mushrooms. Cook on medium-low for 30 minutes. Stir in sherry and cream. Serve with whipped cream and almonds as garnish. Serves 8.

Midwinter Vegetable Chowder

3½ cups chicken broth
1 cup sliced celery
1 cup chopped carrots
2 potatoes, peeled and cut into small pieces
¼ teaspoon pepper
¼ teaspoon salt
1 onion, chopped
One 14-ounce can whole kernel corn
¼ cup butter
¼ cup flour
2 cups milk
2 cups shredded Cheddar cheese

Combine first 7 ingredients in large soup pan; bring to a boil; reduce heat and cook 20 minutes. Remove from heat and add corn. In separate pan melt butter; add flour; cook about 1 minute. Add milk, stirring until thickened; add cheese and stir until blended. Add cheese mixture to vegetable mixture. Serves 6.

Debbie's Green and White Gazpacho

2 cups chicken broth
1¼ cups watercress leaves
2 medium cucumbers, peeled and cut into small pieces
1 green pepper, diced
3 Tablespoons dill
¼ cup mayonnaise
¼ cup sour cream
3 Tablespoons white wine vinegar
2 Tablespoons sugar
½ teaspoon salt
¼ teaspoon pepper

Place all ingredients in blender and process until blended. Serves 4.

Red Tomato Salad

3 cans tomato soup
1⅓ cups crushed pineapple, drained
One 8-ounce package cream cheese
One 3-ounce package cream cheese
½ teaspoon salt
½ medium onion, finely chopped
Red pepper to taste
1 cup whipping cream
1 cup mayonnaise

Place all ingredients in a blender; blend until smooth. Freeze in a 9x13-inch glass baking container. Garnish with greens, olives, etc. Serves 10 to 12.

Hot or Cold Paella

One 5-ounce package saffron rice mix
2 Tablespoons wine vinegar
⅓ cup cooking oil
1⅛ teaspoons dry mustard
Salt to taste
2½ cups cooked, chopped chicken
1 cup chopped, fresh tomatoes
¾ cup chopped green peppers
1 cup cooked green peas
¼ cup chopped onion
⅓ cup chopped celery
One 4-ounce jar pimento, drained
⅓ cup sliced, pitted, ripe olives
⅛ teaspoon Tabasco
½ pound cooked shrimp
1 cup chopped, cooked ham

Cook rice according to directions. Combine vinegar, oil, dry mustard and salt, pour over rice. Place in refrigerator. Mix remaining ingredients together and refrigerate. Add to rice when all is chilled. To serve hot, do not refrigerate after mixing all ingredients.

Dressing

1 cup mayonnaise
1 teaspoon turmeric
½ teaspoon salt
2 Tablespoons lemon juice

Blend and serve in a separate dish.

This can be served hot or cold, either way it is good. Serves 8

Slaw for a Slew

1 head cabbage
1 medium onion
1 or 2 carrots
⅓ cup cooking oil
¾ cup sugar
1 cup vinegar
1 teaspoon salt
1 teaspoon dry mustard
1 teaspoon celery seed

Chop vegetables. Mix remaining ingredients; bring to a boil; pour over cabbage mixture. Refrigerate until serving time.

Party Fleur-de-lis

36 jumbo shrimp, cooked and deveined
6 avocados, cut into wedges
2 grapefruit, sectioned
One 11-ounce can mandarin orange sections, drained
12 cherry tomatoes
1 head red, leaf lettuce

Arrange shrimp and remaining ingredients on lettuce-lined plates. Serve with Remoulade Sauce. Serves 12 as salad or 6 as the main course.

Remoulade Sauce

1 bunch green onions
¼ cup finely-chopped celery
1 clove garlic
¼ cup parsley
⅓ cup white vinegar
3 Tablespoons hot Creole mustard
1 Tablespoon paprika
½ teaspoon salt
¼ teaspoon pepper
⅔ cup olive oil

In food processor, pulse first 4 ingredients until chopped; add vinegar and next 4 ingredients. With processor running add oil in a slow steady stream. Serve over Party Fleur-de-lis.

Santa's Favorite Fajita Salad

¼ cup olive oil
2 Tablespoons lime juice
1 teaspoon oregano
1 teaspoon chili powder
4 boneless pork loin chops, about 1½ pounds
2¼ cups chicken broth
1 cup uncooked, long grain rice
2 ripe avocados, peeled
1 Tablespoon lemon juice
1 medium tomato, chopped
1 jalapeño pepper, chopped
2 Tablespoons chopped parsley
1 Tablespoon chopped onion
1 head iceberg lettuce, finely chopped
One 15-ounce can black beans, rinsed and drained
1 cup shredded, sharp Cheddar cheese
One 11-ounce jar salsa
2 cups sour cream
Olives
Green onions

In large zip lock bag combine first 4 ingredients. Add pork chops, seal and refrigerate for 8 hours, turning occasionally. Grill pork chops for 12-14

minutes until juices run clear. Thinly slice pork; set aside. In saucepan bring chicken broth to boil; stir in rice; reduce heat and simmer for 15 minutes or until rice is tender; cool. Make guacamole by mashing avocados with lemon juice and stirring in tomato, jalapeño, parsley and onion. In a 5-quart glass dish, layer lettuce, beans, cheese, pork and guacamole. Spread with salsa. Combine rice and sour cream; spread over salsa. Garnish with olives and green onions. Serves 6.

Edith's Cranberry Relish

3 oranges, peeled
1 pound package fresh or frozen cranberries
3 apples, cored and cut into eighths
½ cup nuts
2 cups sugar

Cut oranges into eighths. Using a food processor or blender grind cranberries, apples, oranges and nuts. Add sugar; stir to blend. Cover and refrigerate overnight. Makes 1 quart.

Sensational Greek Steak Salad

One 1-pound flank steak
1 cup olive oil
⅓ cup red wine vinegar
2 Tablespoons chopped mint
2 Tablespoons chopped parsley
1 Tablespoon Dijon mustard
1 teaspoon dried oregano
¼ teaspoon salt
¼ teaspoon rosemary
One 14-ounce can artichoke hearts, drained and halved
¼ pound fresh green beans, cut into ½-inch pieces, cooked and chilled
⅓ cup ripe olives, cut in half
1 sweet pepper, cut into thin strips
4 cups torn mixed greens
2 medium tomatoes
½ cup crumbled Feta cheese

Place steak on lightly-greased broiler pan. Broil 4 to 5 inches from heat for
10 to 12 minutes, turning once; cool. Thinly slice steak across grain; set
aside. Combine olive oil and next 7 ingredients in a shallow dish. Add
steak, artichoke hearts, and remaining ingredients except tomatoes and
cheese; cover and refrigerate 3 hours. Arrange greens on a platter; top with
meat mixture; cut tomatoes into wedges; arrange and sprinkle with Feta
cheese. Serves 4.

Cranberry Congealed Chicken Salad

One 3-ounce package lemon gelatin
1½ cups water, divided
½ cup orange juice
One 10-ounce can cranberry sauce without berries
1 package unflavored gelatin
2 cups cooked chopped chicken
2 hard boiled eggs, chopped
½ cup chopped celery
½ cup sliced olives
2 Tablespoons chopped onion
1 cup mayonnaise

Dissolve lemon gelatin in ¾ cup boiling water. Remove from heat; add orange juice and cranberry sauce. Pour into a 9x13-inch glass dish; refrigerate until set. Boil remaining water, dissolve unflavored gelatin; remove from heat. Add remaining ingredients; pour over first layer. Refrigerate until set. Serves 8.

Wilted Cabbage Salad

1 Tablespoon sugar
2 Tablespoons white vinegar
2 Tablespoons water
¼ teaspoon salt
¼ teaspoon pepper
2 slices bacon
⅓ cup chopped onion
1 small cabbage, shredded
1 apple, chopped

Combine first 5 ingredients. In skillet cook bacon; remove from pan; use reserved drippings to sauté onion. Stir in vinegar mixture, cabbage and apple. Cover and cook 5 minutes on medium heat; add crumbled bacon. Serve warm. Serves 4 to 6.

Wild Rice Salad with Cranberries

4 cups cooked white rice
4 cups cooked wild rice
1 cup broken pecan halves
1 cup dried cranberries, soaked in hot water for 10 minutes and drained
1 cup chopped scallion
½ cup finely-chopped celery
1 red pepper, finely chopped
⅓ cup chopped parsley
2 Tablespoons chives
2 Tablespoons dill

Combine ingredients; cover and refrigerate. Serve with dressing.

Dressing

4 Tablespoons rice vinegar or white wine vinegar
4 Tablespoons lemon juice
1 garlic clove, minced
Salt and pepper to taste
½ cup vegetable oil
2 Tablespoons Asian sesame oil

Place ingredients in blender; process on blend. Pour over the salad and toss well. Serves 8 to 10.

Pasta Salad

¼ cup mayonnaise
¼ cup olive oil
1 Tablespoon lemon juice
1½ Tablespoons Greek seasoning
8 ounces cooked vermicelli
One 2-ounce jar diced pimento, drained
One 2¼-ounce can sliced ripe olives, drained
3 green onions, chopped
1 cup cooked, chopped chicken

Blend mayonnaise with next 3 ingredients; add pasta and next 3 ingredients. Stir in chicken. Serves 4.

Cranberry Salad Squares

1½ cups boiling water
One 3-ounce package cherry gelatin
One 3-ounce package orange gelatin
1 cup ground cranberries or one 16-ounce can jellied cranberry sauce
1 unpeeled apple, chopped fine
1 orange, chopped
1 cup orange juice
½ cup sugar

Pour boiling water over gelatin. Add cranberries and stir until dissolved. Add remaining of ingredients; chill. Cut into squares to serve.

Fiesty Cranberry Salsa

3 cups fresh or frozen cranberries
½ purple onion, chopped
2 jalapeño peppers, seeded and chopped
½ cup chopped, fresh cilantro
½ cup honey
2 Tablespoons fresh lime juice
1 Tablespoon grated orange rind

In food processor, chop all ingredients. Cover and chill 8 hours. Makes 2½ cups.

Rudolph's Raspberry Salad

4 cups Boston lettuce
4 cups red leaf lettuce
1 cup walnuts, chopped
1 cup fresh or frozen raspberries
1 avocado, peeled and chopped
1 kiwi fruit, peeled and sliced

Tear lettuces into bite-size pieces. Combine remaining ingredients and serve with Raspberry Salad Dressing. Serves 10.

Raspberry Salad Dressing

⅓ cup raspberry jam
⅓ cup raspberry vinegar
1 cup salad oil
1 Tablespoon poppy seeds

In electric blender process jam, vinegar and oil. Stir in poppy seeds.

Frozen Fruitcake Salad

1 cup sour cream
½ of a 4½-ounce carton frozen whipped topping, thawed
½ cup sugar
2 Tablespoons lemon juice
1 teaspoon vanilla
One 13-ounce can crushed pineapple, drained
2 medium bananas, sliced
½ cup red candied cherries, sliced
½ cup green candied cherries, sliced
½ cup chopped walnuts

Blend sour cream, whipped topping, sugar, lemon juice and vanilla. Fold in fruits and nuts. Freeze overnight. Serves 8 to 12.

Apricot Congealed Salad

One 20-ounce can pineapple tidbits
Two 3-ounce packages apricot gelatin
¼ cup buttermilk
One 12-ounce carton frozen whipped topping, thawed

Drain pineapple, reserving juice. Mix gelatin and juice in saucepan; cook over low heat until dissolved. When cool, add buttermilk, pineapple and whipped topping. Chill overnight. Serves 8 to 12.

Congealed Asparagus Salad

1 can cream of asparagus soup
One 8-ounce package cream cheese
One 3-ounce package lime gelatin
½ cup water
1 Tablespoon chopped onion
½ cup chopped celery
¼ cup chopped green pepper

Combine soup, cream cheese, gelatin and water. Stir in remaining ingredients. Refrigerate until congealed. Serve with asparagus spears and a spoonful of sour cream on the side. Serves 6 to 8.

Cheery Cherry Frozen Salad

1 can cherry pie filling
One 8-ounce can pineapple tidbits, drained
1 can sweetened condensed milk
One 10-ounce carton frozen whipped topping, thawed
1½ cups miniature marshmallows

Mix in large bowl; pour into 9x13-inch dish and freeze. Serve on bed of lettuce. Serves 10 to 14.

Green Goddess Salad Dressing

1 clove garlic
3 Tablespoons chopped green onion
1 Tablespoon lemon juice
3 Tablespoons tarragon white vinegar
½ cup sour cream
1 cup mayonnaise
⅓ cup chopped parsley
Salt and pepper to taste

Mix in order given. Makes 1½ cups.

Honey Mustard Salad Dressing

3 Tablespoons honey
2 Tablespoons Dijon mustard
¼ cup cider vinegar
½ cup vegetable oil

Blend all ingredients in belender. Makes 1 cup.

Blue Cheese Salad Dressing

One 8-ounce carton sour cream
4 Tablespoons lemon juice
4 Tablespoons sugar
1 teaspoon salt
2 Tablespoons mayonnaise
2 ounces blue cheese

Beat until smooth; crumble in blue cheese; mix well. Makes 1½ cups.

Sides

Tennessee Southern Grits Dressing

2 onions, chopped
1 cup chopped celery
¼ cup bacon drippings
1 cup seasoned or stale bread cubes
5 cups crumbled cornbread
1½ cups cooked grits
4 cups chicken or turkey broth
¼ cup butter
3 eggs
1 teaspoon salt
2 to 3 teaspoons poultry seasoning
½ teaspoon pepper

Sauté onion and celery in bacon drippings; blend in remaining ingredients.
Bake in a 9x13-inch greased baking dish at 375 degrees for 30 minutes.
Serves 10.

Traditional Cornbread Stuffing

¾ cup chopped onion
1½ cups chopped celery
1 cup butter
1 Tablespoon poultry seasoning
Salt and pepper to taste
8 cups cornbread crumbs
4 cups chicken or turkey broth
1 box cornbread stuffing mix, prepared according to directions

Sauté onion and celery in butter; add seasonings; remove from heat. In a very large bowl, combine mixture with cornbread crumbs, broth and the stuffing. Bake in a lightly-greased 9x13-inch baking dish or in 2 lightly-greased iron skillets for 45 minutes to 1 hour at 300 degrees. Serves 16 to 20.

Mincemeat Stuffing

One 16-ounce loaf stale French bread
3 Tablespoons butter
1 large onion, chopped
½ cup chopped celery
2 cups prepared mincemeat
½ cup chopped pecans
⅓ cup dry white wine
3 Tablespoons parsley
1 teaspoon sage
1 teaspoon salt
1 teaspoon pepper
2 large eggs, lightly beaten

Cut bread into 1-inch cubes, set aside. Melt butter in large skillet over medium heat. Add chopped onion and celery; sauté until tender. Combine all ingredients; spoon into a lightly-greased 2-quart baking dish. Bake at 350 degrees for 35 to 40 minutes. Serves 6 to 8.

Cranberry Apple Dressing

½ cup chopped onion
2 cups chopped celery
½ cup butter
1 teaspoon thyme
1 teaspoon chopped parsley
1 teaspoon rosemary
2 red tart apples, chopped
1½ cups dried cranberries
1 teaspoon grated orange rind
4 cups unseasoned, dry bread crumbs
1 cup chicken broth

Sauté onion and celery in butter; stir in next 6 ingredients. In large mixing bowl, combine mixture with bread crumbs; add broth. Bake at 350 degrees in a lightly-greased 9x13-inch baking dish covered with foil for 35 to 40 minutes. Serves 6.

Cheddar Cheezy Soufflé

1 cup milk
1 cup shredded Cheddar cheese
2 teaspoons butter
3 slightly-beaten egg yolks
3 stiffly-beaten egg whites
½ cup soft bread crumbs
¼ teaspoon salt
Dash of red pepper

Cook first 3 ingredients in a large saucepan over medium heat, stirring constantly until cheese melts. Stir a small amount of hot mixture into the 3 egg yolks; continue until the hot mixture is blended with the eggs. Add bread crumbs, salt and pepper. Fold beaten egg whites into warm mixture; spoon into a greased 1-quart soufflé dish. Bake at 325 degrees for 50 minutes until lightly browned. Serves 4 to 6.

Tex-Mex Cabbage

1 head cabbage, chopped and boiled about 10 minutes
1 onion, chopped
2 Tablespoons butter
1 Tablespoon sugar
1 green pepper, chopped
One 14½-ounce can chopped tomatoes
¾ cup shredded Cheddar cheese

Place cooked cabbage in a greased 9x13-inch baking dish. Sauté onion in butter; add sugar, pepper and tomatoes. Pour over cabbage; sprinkle with shredded cheese. Bake at 350 degrees for 30 minutes. Serves 8 to 12.

German Red Cabbage

¼ cup sugar
¼ cup brown sugar
½ cup apple cider vinegar
1 medium red cabbage, shredded
2 slices bacon
1 medium apple, chopped
½ cup chopped onion
¼ cup water
2 Tablespoons white wine vinegar
½ teaspoon salt
¼ teaspoon pepper

Combine first 3 ingredients; pour over cabbage. Cook bacon, reserving drippings. Cook apple and onion in bacon drippings until tender; add cabbage mixture and water; bring to boil. Cover, reduce heat and simmer 10 minutes. Add white wine vinegar and salt and pepper to the mixture; simmer uncovered 5 minutes; sprinkle with chopped bacon before serving. Serves 6 to 10.

Spinach in Pasta Shells

Two 10-ounce packages frozen, chopped spinach, thawed
One 15-ounce container Ricotta cheese
1 cup shredded Parmesan, Romano and Asiago cheese blend
1 envelope buttermilk ranch dressing mix
2 lightly-beaten eggs
½ teaspoon pepper
26 jumbo pasta shells, cooked
4 cups marinara sauce
1 cup shredded Mozzarella cheese
2 Tablespoons chopped basil

Drain spinach well, pressing between paper towels. Stir together spinach and next 5 ingredients. Spoon mixture into cooked shells. Spread half of marinara sauce in a lightly-greased 9x13-inch baking dish. Arrange filled shells over sauce; top with remaining sauce. Bake covered at 350 degrees for 40 minutes. Uncover; sprinkle with Mozzarella cheese; bake 5 to 10 minutes longer. Sprinkle with basil. Serves 6 to 8.

My Mississippi Friend's Spinach

Two 10-ounce boxes frozen chopped spinach, cooked and drained
2 cups herb bread stuffing mix
2 onions, finely chopped
6 beaten eggs
½ cup grated Parmesan cheese
¾ cup melted butter
1 Tablespoon garlic salt
½ teaspoon thyme

Mix all ingredients well. Bake in a lightly-greased 9x13-inch baking dish at 350 degrees for 20 minutes. Serves 12.

Turnips on the Table

6 fresh turnips, peeled and cut up
1 Tablespoon butter or 1 teaspoon bacon grease
½ teaspoon sugar
½ teaspoon salt

Cook turnips in water on medium heat until done. While mashing, combine butter, salt and sugar.

Marta's Green Beans

2 cups water
1 pound fresh pole beans, broken and strings removed
1 teaspoon salt
1 whole onion
1 Tablespoon bacon drippings

Bring water to boil; add remaining ingredients; return to boil; reduce heat to medium; cover and cook on medium about 30 minutes until desired doneness. After beans appear done, turn heat to high, stirring constantly until all liquid has boiled out. You may discard the onion and serve. Beef bouillon in place of bacon drippings or a package of onion soup mix may be used for flavoring. Serves 6.

Country Corn Pudding

2 beaten eggs
One 15 to 16-ounce can cream-style corn
One 15 to 16-ounce can whole kernel corn, drained
⅓ cup sugar
¼ cup milk
2 Tablespoons flour
¼ teaspoon salt
Butter

Combine all ingredients except butter. Place in a lightly-greased 8-inch square baking dish, dot with butter. Bake at 350 for about 1 hour. Serves 6.

Corn-Rice Casserole

2 cups uncooked long grain rice
2 Tablespoons butter
1 green pepper, chopped
1 onion, chopped
One 15½-ounce can cream-style corn
One 11-ounce can Mexican style corn, drained
One 11-ounce can whole kernel corn, drained
One 10-ounce can diced tomato and green chilies, undrained
8 ounces mild Mexican pasteurized prepared cheese product, cubed
Dash of salt and pepper
½ cup shredded Cheddar cheese

Cook rice according to package directions. Sauté in butter the bell pepper and onion for 5 minutes. Stir in cooked rice and remaining ingredients except shredded cheese. Place in a lightly-greased 3½-quart baking dish. Bake 350 degrees for 30 minutes; top with shredded Cheddar cheese and bake 5 additional minutes. Serves 10 to 12.

Asparagus Casserole

1 can mushroom soup
2 cans asparagus, drained
½ stick butter
½ cup cracker crumbs
½ cup slivered almonds
½ cup grated cheese

Pour mushroom soup over asparagus in a baking dish. Add melted butter and cracker crumbs. Add almonds and top with cheese. Bake at 375 degrees for 20 minutes. Serves 6.

Hot Cranberries

2 cups raw cranberries
3 cups peeled and chopped apples
1 cup sugar
1 stick butter
1 cup uncooked quick-cooking oats
1 cup brown sugar

Toss first 3 ingredients and place in a lightly-greased 9x9-inch baking dish. Top with mixture of the remaining 3 ingredients. Bake at 350 degrees for 1 hour. Serves 8 to 10.

Mrs. Santa's Sweet Potato Soufflé

One 14½-ounce can sweet potatoes
1 cup sugar
¼ cup milk
1 teaspoon grated orange rind
2 Tablespoons orange juice
1 teaspoon vanilla
2 eggs, lightly beaten
⅔ cup flour, divided
½ cup butter, divided
1 cup pecans, chopped
1 cup brown sugar

Mash potatoes; add next 6 ingredients to mashed potatoes; add ⅓ cup of the flour and ¼ cup butter. Pour into a lightly-buttered 9x13-inch baking dish. Sprinkle over this a mixture of the pecans, brown sugar, ⅓ cup flour and ¼ cup butter. Bake at 350 for 45 minutes. Serves 10 to 12.

Sweet Potatoes for the Elves

6 oranges
2 pounds cooked mashed sweet potatoes
1 stick butter, melted
3 eggs, beaten
¾ cup sugar
1 cup brown sugar
1 teaspoon cinnamon
½ teaspoon nutmeg
1 teaspoon vanilla
1 cup orange juice
12 large marshmallows

Cut oranges in half; squeeze juice and remove pulp, making 12 orange peel cups. Add enough orange juice to equal 1 cup. Combine mashed potatoes with butter and eggs with electric mixer. Add sugars, spices, vanilla and orange juice. Place in 12 orange peel cups. Set in muffin tins. Bake at 375 degrees for 30-45 minutes; place large marshmallow on top of each orange cup; return to oven and brown. Serves 12.

Supreme Broccoli

Two 10-ounce packages frozen chopped broccoli
1 cup baking mix
1 cup milk
2 eggs
½ teaspoon salt
1 cup shredded Cheddar cheese

Cook broccoli as directed; drain. Mix baking mix, milk, eggs and salt; stir in broccoli and cheese. Pour into a buttered soufflé dish or 1½-quart casserole dish. Bake at 325 degrees for 1 hour or until knife inserted halfway comes out clean. Serves 6.

Easy Parmesan-Paprika Oven Baked Potatoes

¾ cup grated Parmesan cheese
⅓ cup flour
3 Tablespoons paprika
½ teaspoon pepper
8 small baking potatoes
½ cup butter, melted

Place first 4 ingredients in a zip-lock bag; shake to blend. Cut potatoes into about 8 slices each; place in bag and shake to cover; place in a 9x13-inch baking dish and drizzle melted butter over. Bake at 375 degrees for 20 minutes, turning once, until done. Serves 6.

Elegant French Onion Special

3 medium onions, sliced crosswise and cut in half
One 8-ounce package sliced mushrooms
2 Tablespoons butter
2 cups shredded Swiss cheese, divided
One can cream of mushroom soup
One 5-ounce can evaporated milk
2 teaspoons soy sauce
6 slices French bread
¼ cup chopped parsley

Sauté onions and mushrooms in butter until tender. Place in a greased 2-quart baking dish; sprinkle with 1 cup of cheese. Combine soup, milk and soy sauce; pour over cheese. Top with bread slices; sprinkle with remaining 1 cup of cheese and parsley. Cover and refrigerate 6 to 8 hours. Remove from refrigerator let stand at room temperature 30 minutes. Bake covered at 375 degrees for 30 minutes, uncover and bake an additional 15 minutes. Serves 6.

Minnie's Greens

½ pound salt pork or smoked pork shoulder
2 quarts water
One 16-ounce bag frozen collard greens
One 16-ounce bag frozen turnip greens
¼ teaspoon pepper
Pinch of sugar

Slice salt pork or shoulder, but do not cut through the skin. Bring to boil in water in a large Dutch oven or heavy pan with a lid; simmer at least 1 hour. Add greens and cook 20 to 40 minutes; add pepper and a pinch of sugar. When serving, have hot sauce or vinegar available to sprinkle on top. Serves 4.

Carrot Casserole

8 cups sliced carrots
1 onion, chopped
1 Tablespoon butter
1 can cream of mushroom soup
One 4-ounce can mushrooms, drained
½ cup grated Parmesan cheese
1 cup soft bread crumbs

Cook carrots in water until tender; drain. In skillet, sauté onion in butter; add carrots, soup, mushrooms and Parmesan cheese. Place in a lightly-greased 2½-quart baking dish. Sprinkle with bread crumbs. Bake uncovered at 350 degrees for 30 minutes. Serves 10 to 12.

Dancer's Dessert Carrots

1 pound of carrots, peeled, cut and cooked
1 stick butter
1 teaspoon baking powder
½ teaspoon cinnamon
3 Tablespoons flour
1 cup sugar
3 well-beaten eggs

Mash carrots with butter; add dry ingredients. Add beaten eggs. Pour into a lightly-greased 8x8 or 9x9-inch baking dish. Bake at 350 degrees for 1 hour and 15 minutes. Serves 6 to 10.

Company Corn Flan

2½ cups fresh or frozen whole kernel corn, thawed
1½ cups whipping cream
4 eggs
½ teaspoon salt
¼ teaspoon hot sauce
3 Tablespoons shredded Monterey Jack cheese
⅓ cup chopped fresh or frozen chives

Combine first 5 ingredients in container of an electric blender; process until smooth. Stir in cheese and chopped chives. Pour mixture into 6 lightly-greased 8-ounce ramekins. Place ramekins in a large pan. Add hot water to pan to depth of 1 inch. Cover pan with foil. Bake at 325 degrees for 45 to 50 minutes or until a knife inserted in center comes out clean. Unmold and garnish with chives, if desired. Serves 6.

Entrées

Kid's Favorite Beef Enchiladas

24 corn tortillas
1 cup hot salad oil
2 pounds ground beef
2 Tablespoons chili powder
3 Tablespoons Worcestershire
1 Tablespoon grated onion
1 teaspoon hot sauce
1 cup chopped onion
2 pounds Monterey Jack cheese, sliced
Three 10-ounce cans tomatoes with green chilies
1 teaspoon minced garlic

Fry tortillas in hot salad oil; drain. Brown ground beef; add chili powder, Worcestershire, grated onion and hot sauce. Spoon 2 tablespoons mixture on each tortilla; top with chopped onion and slice of cheese, reserving some of each for top. Roll tightly and arrange in a greased 9x13-inch baking dish. Combine tomatoes with green chilies with garlic in saucepan; simmer 10 minutes. Pour sauce over enchiladas; top with reserved chopped onions and sliced cheese. Bake at 350 degrees for 20 minutes. Serves 8 to 10.

Church Supper Beef Casserole

½ cup chopped onion
1½ pounds ground beef
One 12-ounce can whole kernel corn, drained
One 11-ounce can Cheddar cheese soup, undiluted
1 cup sour cream
¼ cup chopped pimento
½ teaspoon salt
½ teaspoon pepper
3 cups cooked noodles, drained
Cracker crumbs
½ cup shredded Cheddar cheese
3 Tablespoons butter

Sauté onion and ground beef until brown; add corn, soup, sour cream, pimento, salt, pepper and noodles. Spoon into a lightly-greased 9x13-inch baking dish. Sprinkle with cracker crumbs and cheese. Dot with butter. Bake at 350 degrees for 30 minutes. Serves 6 to 8.

Evelyn's Chili

1 pound ground beef
1 cup chopped onion
1 teaspoon garlic powder
2 Tablespoons chili powder
One 46-ounce can tomato juice
2 or 3 cans chili beans or kidney beans
¼ pound uncooked spaghetti
1 can tamales, optional
Worcestershire sauce

Brown ground beef and onion in a large Dutch oven; add garlic powder and chili powder. Add remaining ingredients. Cook on low heat until spaghetti is done. Best if cooked at least 1 hour.

Delightful Christmas Party Beef Tenderloin

1 cup catsup
2 teaspoons prepared mustard
1 teaspoon Worcestershire sauce
1½ cups water
Two 0.7-ounce envelopes Italian salad dressing mix
One 4 to 6-pound beef tenderloin, trimmed

Combine first 5 ingredients; mix well. Spear meat in several places, place in a zip-top bag, pour in marinade and seal. Refrigerate overnight, turning bag over occasionally. Drain off and reserve marinade. Place tenderloin on rack in baking pan. Bake at 425 degrees for 30 to 45 minutes or or until meat thermometer registers 140 degrees for rare. Bake to 150 degrees for medium rare. Baste occasionally with marinade while baking. Remove to serving platter; serve remaining marinade with tenderloin. Serves 12 to 15.

Chicken Divan for All Seasons

Two 10-ounce packages frozen broccoli spears
6 cooked chicken breasts, chopped
Garlic salt and butter to taste
One 10-ounce can cream of chicken soup
1 cup sour cream
3 Tablespoons milk
1 cup grated Cheddar cheese
3 Tablespoons sherry or cooking sherry
Toasted almonds

Cook broccoli according to package directions. Place layer of broccoli and layer of chicken in a casserole. Sprinkle with garlic salt; dot with butter. Combine soup, sour cream, milk, Cheddar cheese and sherry. Pour half of mixture over chicken; repeat layers. Sprinkle with almonds. Bake at 375 degrees for 45 minutes. Serves 6.

Creamed Chicken with Cornbread Waffles

½ cup butter
½ cup flour
1 teaspoon salt
2 cups chicken broth
2 cups half & half
2 cups milk
4 cups chopped, cooked chicken
One 8-ounce can sliced water chestnuts, drained
½ jar pimento, drained and chopped
¼ cup sherry

Melt butter; add flour and salt; stir until smooth; add chicken broth, half & half and milk; stir again until smooth. Simmer 30 minutes. Add remaining ingredients and heat thoroughly. Serve over Cornbread Waffles, regular cornbread or in pastry shells.

Cornbread Waffles

1½ cups cornmeal
½ cup flour
2½ teaspoons baking powder
2 Tablespoons sugar
½ teaspoon salt
1 egg
1½ cups milk
¼ cup butter, melted
1½ cups frozen white shoepeg corn, thawed

Stir together first 5 ingredients in large bowl. In another bowl stir together remaining ingredients; add to cornmeal mixture, stirring until dry ingredients are moistened. Bake in preheated, oiled waffle iron until crisp. Makes 12 waffles.

Christmas Celebration Chicken Cheesecakes

1½ cups packed, fresh basil leaves
½ cup chopped pecans
½ cup olive oil
3 garlic cloves
3 Tablespoons lemon juice
¼ teaspoon salt
Two 8-ounce packages cream cheese, softened
2 eggs
3 Tablespoons flour, divided
1 cup chopped, cooked chicken
One 8-ounce container sour cream
Mixed salad greens

Make 1 cup of pesto by blending first 6 ingredients in a food processor or blender until smooth. Place 3 tablespoons of pesto in a large mixing bowl; refrigerate remainder for future use.   Using an electric mixer, beat pesto, cream cheese, eggs and two tablespoons flour until blended. Stir in chicken. Pour into a lightly-greased 9-inch spring-form pan. Bake at 325 degrees for 25 minutes.   Blend together sour cream and 1 tablespoon flour; spread over cheesecake and bake an additional 15 minutes. Cool on wire rack 10 minutes. Serves 4, hot or cold, on top of salad greens.

Mike's Stir-Fry Chicken

3 Tablespoons soy sauce
2 teaspoons cornstarch
2 Tablespoons dry sherry
1 teaspoon sugar
1 teaspoon grated, fresh ginger
½ teaspoon red pepper
¼ teaspoon salt
2 Tablespoons vegetable oil
2 green bell peppers, sliced into strips
4 or 5 green onions, sliced or 1 regular onion, sliced
5 chicken breasts, boned and sliced into 1-inch pieces
½ cup chopped English walnuts

Mix together soy sauce, cornstarch, sherry, sugar, ginger, red pepper and salt. Place oil in wok over high heat; stir-fry green peppers and onions until tender; remove. Add half of chicken pieces and stir-fry for 2 or 3 minutes; remove and add remaining chicken and stir-fry for 2 or 3 minutes. Return all chicken to the wok. Stir soy mixture and add to chicken; cook and stir until bubbly. Add vegetables and walnuts; cover and cook for 1 minute. Serve with cooked rice. Serves 6.

Meridith's White Lasagna for a Christmas Buffet

1 onion, chopped
2 Tablespoons butter
2 Tablespoons flour
2 cups chicken broth
1 package Alfredo sauce mix, prepared according to package directions or
One 10-ounce jar prepared Alfredo sauce
One 10-ounce box frozen, chopped spinach, thawed and well drained
12 lasagna noodles, cooked in salted water
One 8-ounce package sliced Mozzarella cheese
One 8-ounce container Ricotta or cottage cheese
3 cups chopped, cooked chicken breast
Parmesan cheese

Sauté onion in butter; add flour, stirring until blended. Slowly add chicken broth; mix until blended and slightly thickened. Combine with Alfredo sauce. Add spinach. Spoon small amount of sauce to cover the bottom in a lightly-greased 9x13-inch baking dish. Layer noodles, cheeses, chicken and sauce, finishing with sauce on top. Sprinkle with Parmesan cheese. Bake at 350 degrees for 30 to 45 minutes. Serves 8 to 10.

Prize - Winning White Chili

1 pound white beans, cooked
4 chicken breasts
2 cups chicken broth
1 onion, chopped
1 Tablespoon butter
1 can cream of mushroom soup
2 Tablespoons chili powder
1 teaspoon garlic salt
1 teaspoon salt
½ teaspoon pepper
Sour cream and salsa for garnish

In large pan, cook chicken breasts in broth until done. Remove from broth; pull or cut into bite-size portions. Sauté onion in butter, add beans, chicken, soup and remaining ingredients, except sour cream and salsa. Cook until hot. Serve with a spoonful each of sour cream and salsa on top. Serves 6 to 8.

Cranberry Chicken with Walnuts

4 cups chopped, cooked chicken
2 cups chopped celery
2 cups fresh or frozen cranberries
1 cup chopped walnuts
1 can cream of chicken soup
1 cup mayonnaise
2 cups cooked rice
2 green onions, chopped
6 hard boiled eggs, chopped
½ cup buttered bread crumbs

Combine all ingredients except bread crumbs. Place in a buttered 9x13-inch baking dish; top with bread crumbs. Bake at 350 degrees for 20 minutes. Serves 8 to 10.

Pork Tenderloin with Cranberries

One 1-pound pork tenderloin, cut into ½-inch slices
3 Tablespoons olive or vegetable oil
1 onion, chopped
1 clove garlic, finely chopped
4 Tablespoons sugar
¾ cup apple juice
½ cup cranberry juice
½ cup fresh or frozen cranberries
2 teaspoons Dijon mustard
½ teaspoon rosemary

Cook pork in oil for 3 to 4 minutes until browned. Remove pork from heat. In same skillet sauté onion, garlic and sugar until onion is caramelized. Stir in apple and cranberry juices, cranberries, mustard and rosemary. Bring to a boil; add pork; reduce heat and simmer covered for 30 minutes.

Tennessee Whole Country Ham

One 12 to 14-pound uncooked country ham
2 quarts cider vinegar
1 Tablespoon cloves

Place ham in a large container. Add water to cover and soak 24 hours.
Drain and place ham fat-side-up in a large roasting pan. Pour vinegar
over ham; sprinkle with cloves. Cover with lid or aluminum foil. Bake at
320 degrees for 4 hours or until meat thermometer registers 140 degrees.
Remove from oven and cool slightly before slicing. Serves 35.

Sesame Flounder

Eight 4-ounce flounder fillets or other firm white fish
1 teaspoon lemon juice
¼ teaspoon pepper
½ cup diced onion
½ cup diced green pepper
½ cup diced celery
¼ cup frozen apple juice concentrate, thawed
2 teaspoons toasted sesame seeds

Butter or use vegetable cooking spray to cover bottom of a 9x13-inch baking dish. Place fillets in dish; drizzle with lemon juice; sprinkle with pepper. Sauté onion, green pepper and celery in apple juice until crisp-tender; spoon over fillets. Sprinkle with sesame seeds and bake at 350 degrees for 25 minutes or until fish flakes easily. Serves 8.

Lobster Newburg

1 cup sliced mushrooms
1 pound fresh or frozen lobster
4 Tablespoons butter
½ cup sherry
1½ cups heavy cream
½ teaspoon salt
¼ teaspoon cayenne pepper
2 egg yolks, beaten
1 Tablespoon flour
¼ cup water

Sauté mushrooms and lobster in melted butter for 3 minutes; add sherry; cover and simmer for 3 minutes. Add cream, salt and pepper; simmer 10 minutes. Add ½ cup of the cream mixture to the egg yolks; return to pan; add flour dissolved in water. Heat thoroughly, but do not boil. Serve over cooked rice, on toast points, or in patty shells. Serves 6.

Catfish Dinner

8 ounces catfish fillets
1 sweet red bell pepper, cut into strips
1 carrot, cut into strips
1 zucchini, cut into strips
3 Tablespoons butter, melted
One 14-ounce can artichoke hearts, drained and cut into quarters
⅔ cup whipping cream
8 ounces angel hair pasta, cooked and drained
½ cup grated, Parmesan cheese

Cut fillets into 2-inch strips; set aside. Sauté red pepper, carrot and zucchini in butter until tender. Remove vegetables from skillet, add catfish and sauté until tender. Return vegetables to skillet; add artichokes and whipping cream Cook over low heat until heated. Add pasta and cheese; toss gently. Serves 4.

Veal Scallopini with Fettuccine

1⅓ pounds veal, thinly sliced
Flour, salt and pepper
½ cup butter
¼ cup Marsala wine
3 Tablespoons canned beef bouillon concentrate

Pound veal until thin; dip in flour, seasoned with salt and pepper. Heat butter in heavy skillet; add veal and brown. Add wine and cook 1 minute longer. Remove meat to warm serving dish. Add bouillon to pan drippings; bring to boil and pour over meat. Serves 4.

Fettuccine

1 stick butter
½ cup Parmesan cheese
½ pint whipping cream, whipped
1 pound noodles, cooked according to directions

Melt butter; add cheese and whipped cream. Add hot cooked noodles and serve.

Leg of Lamb

One 5 to 6-pound leg of lamb
6 garlic cloves
6 springs of rosemary

Cut slits into leg of lamb. Insert a garlic clove and sprig of rosemary in each slit. Place lamb on a rack in a roasting pan. Bake at 450 degrees for 5 minutes; decrease temperature to 350 degrees and bake 1½ hours until meat thermometer registers 145 degrees for medium rare. Remove lamb from oven and let stand 15 minutes before carving. Serves 6 to 8.

Duck with Cherry Sauce

One 4 to 5-pound duck
One 12-ounce jar cherry preserves
1½ Tablespoons red wine vinegar

Prick skin of duck well and place breast-side-up on a rack in a roasting pan. Tie drumsticks together. Bake uncovered at 325 degrees for approximately 2 hours (180 on meat thermometer). Cover and let stand for 20 minutes before carving. Combine and heat cherry preserves and red wine vinegar for sauce to serve with the duck. Serves 4 to 6.

Turkey in the Oven

Rinse turkey in cold water; remove giblets; sprinkle with salt; place several slices of butter over the bird. Wrap in foil and bake at 325 degrees for 4 to 6 hours.   Refer to directions on turkey packages for cooking times for various sizes.

Turkey in a Bag

Rinse turkey in cold water; remove giblets; rub with cooking oil. Place in a big brown grocery sack and tie with a string. Place on a cooking pan and roast in 300-degree oven for 30 minutes per pound for a 7 to 10-pound turkey, 20 minutes per pound for a 10 to 15-pound turkey, or 15 minutes per pound for an 18 to 20-pound turkey.

Smoked Turkey

Rinse and salt turkey. On electric smoker, place 3 to 4 wooden chips on burner. Use mesquite, hickory or any flavor chips desired. Place a pan of water over the burner and the turkey on a rack above the water. Cover with the lid of smoker and cook 8 to 12 hours, depending on the size of turkey. Cooking your turkey outside frees up your oven for other baking, plus it is delicious.

Desserts

Pumpkin Spice Dessert

1 cup biscuit mix
½ cup quick-cooking oats, uncooked
1 cup brown sugar, divided
¼ cup plus 2 Tablespoons butter, divided
One 16-ounce can pumpkin
One 13-ounce can evaporated milk
2 eggs
¾ cup plus 1 tablespoon sugar, divided
½ teaspoon salt
1½ teaspoons cinnamon, divided
½ cup chopped pecans
1 cup whipped cream
1 teaspoon grated orange peel

Mix biscuit mix, oats, ½ cup brown sugar and ¼ cup butter; press in either a 9x13-inch or jelly roll pan. Bake at 350 degrees for 10 minutes. Beat together pumpkin, milk, eggs, ¾ cup sugar, salt and 1 teaspoon cinnamon. Pour over baked layer. Bake at 350 degrees for 20 minutes. Mix pecans, remaining ½ cup brown sugar and 2 tablespoons butter. Sprinkle over filling. Bake at 350 degrees for 15 to 20 minutes. Combine whipped cream, 1 tablespoon sugar, orange peel and cinnamon for dessert topping. Serves 12 to 16.

Pilgrim Pumpkin Pie

1½ cups confectioner's sugar
One 8-ounce package cream cheese, softened
4 Tablespoons butter, softened
1 Tablespoon vanilla
1 teaspoon pumpkin pie spice
One 16-ounce can pumpkin
One 9-inch graham cracker pie crust
1 pint whipping cream, whipped
¼ cup sugar

Mix with an electric mixer confectioner's sugar, cream cheese, butter, vanilla and pumpkin pie spice until fluffy. Blend in pumpkin; spoon into piecrust; chill overnight. Whip cream in electric mixer, adding sugar slowly, until stiff peaks are formed. Use to top dessert. Serves 8.

White Chocolate Chip Cookies with Macadamia Nuts

½ cup butter, softened
½ cup packed brown sugar
2 Tablespoons sugar
1 large egg
2 teaspoons vanilla
2 cups flour
¾ teaspoon baking soda
½ teaspoon baking powder
Pinch of salt
One 6-ounce package vanilla-milk morsels or
1 cup white chocolate baking bar chunks
One 7-ounce jar macadamia nuts, chopped

Using an electric mixer beat butter; add sugars, egg and vanilla. Combine flour, baking soda, baking powder and salt; add to butter mixture mixing well. Stir in white chocolate and nuts. Drop by teaspoonfuls onto lightly-greased cookie sheet. Bake at 350 degrees for 8 to 10 minutes until lightly browned. Cool on wire racks. Makes 5 dozen.

Kid's Treat Cookie Press Cookies

1 cup butter
1 cup sugar
1½ teaspoons vanilla
2 eggs
3 cups flour, sifted
¼ teaspoon salt

Cream butter, sugar and vanilla; add eggs. Add flour and salt. Cover and chill dough for about 1 hour. Separate dough into 3 or 4 parts. Add food coloring if desired. Press through cookie press onto an ungreased cookie sheet. Bake at 400 degrees for 10 to 12 minutes. While cooling on rack, add sprinkles if desired.

Little Elves Cranberry-Almond Cookies

1 cup butter, softened
¾ cup sugar
¾ cup light brown sugar
½ teaspoon almond extract
2 eggs
2¼ cups flour
1 teaspoon baking powder
½ teaspoon salt
2 cups chopped fresh or frozen cranberries
1 cup slivered almonds

Using an electric mixer cream butter; add sugars, almond extract and eggs. In a separate bowl combine flour, baking powder and salt. Add to butter mixture. Stir in cranberries and almonds. Drop by rounded tablespoonfuls onto an ungreased baking sheet. Bake at 375 degrees for 9 to 11 minutes; cool on a wire rack. Makes 36 cookies.

Lemon Yum Yum Cookies

1¼ cups flour
½ cup cornstarch
⅓ cup powdered sugar
1½ sticks butter, softened
1 Tablespoon lemon juice

Mix all ingredients with electric mixer; divide dough in half and shape into long rolls. Wrap in plastic wrap and refrigerate about 2 hours. Remove from refrigerator and slice ¼-inch cookies; place on an ungreased cookie sheet about 2 inches apart. Bake at 350 degrees for 8 to 12 minutes. Do not brown. Cool and frost. Makes 3 dozen.

Frosting

¾ cup powdered sugar
½ stick butter, softened
1 teaspoon lemon juice

Mix together with electric mixer. Frost cookies.

My Mom's Fruitcake Cookies

1 pound pecans, chopped
1 pound candied cherries, chopped
1 pound walnuts, chopped
1 pound candied pineapple, chopped
1 pound dates, chopped
3 cups flour, divided
½ pound butter, melted
3 eggs
1¾ cups sugar
¾ cup water
½ teaspoon soda
1 teaspoon nutmeg
1 teaspoon allspice
1 teaspoon vanilla
1 teaspoon lemon juice
3 teaspoons cinnamon

Combine first 5 ingredients; cover with ½ cup of flour. Mix together butter, eggs, sugar and water. To butter mixture add 2½ cups flour and remaining ingredients; pour over chopped fruit and nuts. Drop by teaspoons onto lightly-greased cookie sheet. Bake at 275 degrees 15 to 20 minutes. Makes 12 to 14 dozen.

Apple Goody

3 cups sliced apples, peeled (not Red Delicious)
1 cup sugar
¾ cup plus 1 Tablespoon flour, divided
Pinch of salt
1½ teaspoons cinnamon
¾ cup uncooked oatmeal
¾ cup flour
¾ cup brown sugar
½ teaspoon baking soda
¼ teaspoon baking powder
⅓ cup melted butter

Mix together apples, sugar, 1 tablespoon flour and salt and place in a baking pan. Mix together the remaining ingredients and pat over apple mixture. Bake at 350 degrees for 30 minutes. Serve with whipped cream or ice cream.

Freshly Baked Apple Cake

2 eggs
1 cup white sugar
1 cup brown sugar
1¼ cup cooking oil
Pinch of salt
3 cups flour
1 teaspoon soda
1 teaspoon cinnamon
2 teaspoons vanilla
1 cup chopped pecans
3 cups chopped and peeled apples

Mix all but last 2 ingredients in the order listed. Add apples and nuts. Bake in a floured and greased tube pan at 350 degrees for 1 hour and 15 minutes.

Aunt Bessie's Blueberry Pie

One unbaked 9-inch pie crust
Chopped pecans
2 cups blueberries
½ cup sugar
¾ cup water
3 Tablespoons cornstarch in small amount of water
One 8-ounce package cream cheese, softened
1½ cups powdered sugar
One 8-ounce carton frozen whipped topping, thawed

Push pecans into the piecrust; bake at 350 degrees 10 to 15 minutes until lightly browned. Bring berries, sugar and ¾ cup water to a boil, remove immediately before berries burst. Mix cornstarch in water and pour into berry mixture, stirring until clear. Mix together cream cheese and powdered sugar; add whipped topping and spoon mixture into piecrust. Spoon berries over top and cover with plastic wrap. Refrigerate until set. Makes 2 pies, one to share and one to eat.

Tipsy Bread Pudding with Coconut Sauce

8 slices sandwich bread, trimmed and torn into small 1-inch pieces
Two 3-ounce packages cream cheese, softened
1 cup light brown sugar, packed
6 eggs
1 cup milk
Two 8-ounce cans crushed pineapple, drained
2 cups flaked coconut

Bake bread pieces at 375 degrees for 10 to 12 minutes. Using an electric mixer, beat cream cheese; add sugar and eggs. Stir in milk, pineapple and coconut. Fold in bread pieces. Spoon into a lightly-greased 1½-quart baking dish. Bake at 375 degrees for 30 minutes. Serve with Coconut Sauce. Serves 8.

Coconut Sauce

1 cup cream of coconut
One 8-ounce container sour cream
1 Tablespoon rum

Strain cream of coconut; add sour cream and rum, if desired. Makes 2 cups.

Winter Bread Pudding with Bourbon Sauce

3 Tablespoons butter, melted
¾ cup sugar
2 cups milk
3 eggs
2 teaspoons vanilla
Three 1-inch-thick French bread slices, torn into small pieces

Drizzle butter into an 8-inch square pan. In a bowl mix together sugar, milk, eggs and vanilla; add bread. Spoon mixture into pan. Bake at 350 degrees for 15 minutes; stir and bake another 30 minutes. Best served with Bourbon Sauce. Serves 4 to 6.

Bourbon Sauce

1 cup whipping cream
1 teaspoon vanilla
3 egg yolks
⅓ cup sugar
3 Tablespoons bourbon

In saucepan, heat whipping cream and vanilla. Beat together egg yolks and sugar; add to hot mixture. Cook over low heat for 3 minutes; cook and stir 2 more minutes; remove from heat and add bourbon.

Betty's Easy Pie Crust

1 cup flour
⅓ cup cooking oil
3 Tablespoons milk

Place all ingredients directly into a 9-inch pie pan. Stir to form a ball. Press dough to shape of pie pan. Prick with a fork. If your recipe calls for an unbaked crust, bake at 350 degrees for 3 to 4 minutes to set, so the the bottom is not soggy, then fill.

Debbie's Chess Pie

1 stick butter
1½ cups sugar
1½ teaspoons cornmeal
1½ teaspoons vinegar
3 eggs, slightly beaten
1 teaspoon vanilla
One unbaked 9-inch pie crust

Mix butter, sugar, cornmeal and vinegar in pan over low heat until butter is melted. Remove from heat. Add eggs and vanilla. Pour into unbaked pie shell and bake at 325 degrees for 40 to 45 minutes.

Christmas Cheer Cheesecake

1¼ cups salted pretzel crumbs
¾ cup plus 1 Tablespoon sugar, divided
½ cup butter
Two 8-ounce packages cream cheese, softened
2 individual size envelopes instant Margarita mix
4 eggs
⅓ cup tequila
1½ teaspoons grated lime rind, divided
1 teaspoon vanilla
Two 8-ounce cartons sour cream
1 Tablespoon fresh lime juice

Combine pretzel crumbs, 1 tablespoon sugar and butter. Press into a 9-inch spring-form pan. Bake at 375 degrees for 6 to 8 minutes. Using an electric mixer beat cream cheese, adding ½ cup sugar and Margarita mix. Add eggs; stir in tequila, 1 teaspoon lime rind and vanilla. Pour into prepared pan. Bake at 375 degrees for 25 to 30 minutes. Combine sour cream, ½ cup sugar, ½ teaspoon grated lime rind and lime juice. Spread over top of the cheesecake. Bake at 425 degrees for 10 minutes. Cover and chill for 8 hours. Serves 6 to 9.

Chocolate Pound Cake
From Good to Sinful

1 cup butter, softened
1 cup shortening
3 cups sugar
5 eggs
3 cups flour
¼ cup cocoa
½ teaspoon baking powder
¼ teaspoon salt
1 cup milk
2 teaspoons vanilla

Using an electric mixer beat butter and shortening until creamy; add sugar; add eggs. In separate bowl blend flour, cocoa, baking powder and salt. Add to butter mixture, alternating with the milk. Stir in vanilla. Pour into a greased and floured tube pan. Bake at 325 degrees for 1½ hours. Cool on a wire rack 10 to 15 minutes before removing from pan. This may be served plain, with whipped cream or with Hot Fudge Sauce and vanilla ice cream to make one of those "to die for" desserts.

Hot Fudge Sauce

¼ cup cocoa
1¼ cups sugar
1 cup water
1 can sweetened condensed milk
1 teaspoon vanilla
Pinch of salt

Boil together cocoa, sugar and water for 5 minutes. Add condensed milk. Cook 20 minutes on low heat. Add vanilla and salt.

Joyful Pear Jam Cake

1 cup butter
2½ cups sugar
4 eggs
1 teaspoon vanilla
3¼ cups flour
¾ teaspoon baking soda
1 teaspoon cinnamon
1 teaspoon ground cloves
1 teaspoon ground allspice
1 cup buttermilk
One 11½-ounce jar pear preserves
1 cup chopped pecans
Powdered sugar for topping

Using an electric mixer beat butter and sugar until fluffy. Add eggs and vanilla. In a separate bowl combine flour and next 4 ingredients. Add this mixture to the butter mixture alternating with the buttermilk. Beat at low speed until blended. Fold in pear preserves and pecans. Pour into a greased and floured tube pan. Bake at 325 degrees for 1 hour and 20 minutes. Cool for 10 minutes on a wire rack before removing from pan. Sprinkle top with powdered sugar.

Michael's Coconut Cake

1 box white cake mix, baked according to directions for 2 layers
1 large fresh coconut
2 egg whites
½ cups sugar
¼ teaspoon cream of tartar
⅓ cup water
1 teaspoon vanilla

Place a large nail or ice pick in soft eye of the coconut to open and let coconut milk drain into a cup. On cooled cake punch holes with a fork; spoon coconut milk over tops of layers so it soaks into the cake. Using a hammer, break coconut into several pieces. Place pieces on a cookie sheet and into a heated oven for about 10 minutes to help in the removal of the coconut shell. Remove shell, peel off brown skin; cut coconut into small pieces and place small amounts at a time in a blender or food processor to grate. Reserve grated coconut.

For icing mix remaining ingredients, except grated coconut and vanilla in the top of a double boiler. Place over boiling water and beat with an electric mixer on medium-low speed until stiff peaks form. Scrape bottom and sides of pan occasionally. Fold in vanilla. Frost cake and place grated coconut over the frosting. Keep chilled.

Tennessee Blackberry Jam Cake

1 cup butter
2 cups sugar
4 eggs
3 cups flour
2 teaspoons baking powder
1 teaspoon salt
1 teaspoon cinnamon
1 cup milk
One 10 to 12-ounce jar blackberry jam
¾ cup chopped nuts

Cream butter, sugar and eggs. Combine flour, baking powder, salt and cinnamon. Alternate dry ingredients with milk into creamed mixture; add jam and nuts. Bake in a well-greased and floured stem pan at 350 degrees for 1 hour and 15 minutes. Cool and frost.

Frosting

½ stick butter
One 16-ounce box powdered sugar
1 egg white, unbeaten
2 to 3 Tablespoons sherry

Using an electric mixer, blend butter, sugar and egg white; add sherry; beat until smooth.

Something Special Raspberries Mold

1½ cups sugar
2 envelopes unflavored gelatin
1 cup cold water
2 cups whipping cream
Three 8-ounce cartons sour cream
2 teaspoons vanilla

Combine sugar, gelatin and water in saucepan. Cook over medium heat until gelatin dissolves. Stir in whipping cream and set aside. Combine sour cream and vanilla; stir in whipping cream mixture until blended. Pour into a lightly-oiled 7-cup mold; cover and chill overnight. Unmold onto serving dish. Spoon Raspberry Sauce on top.

Raspberry Sauce

One 10-ounce package frozen raspberries, thawed
2 Tablespoons sugar
1 Tablespoon raspberry liqueur

Blend all with electric mixer or blender. Strain to remove seeds, if desired. Spoon sauce over dessert.

Swedish Fruit Bars

1 cup butter, melted
6 Tablespoons powdered sugar
2½ cups flour, divided
4 eggs, beaten
2 cups sugar
1 teaspoon baking powder
1 teaspoon vanilla
1½ cups chopped pecans
1 cup coconut
Three 4-ounce containers candied cherries, chopped

Cream butter and powdered sugar; add 2 cups flour. Pat in jellyroll-size pan with fingers or spoon and bake for 25 minutes at 350 degrees. Mix remaining ingredients and spread over crust. Bake an additional 25 minutes at 350 degrees. Cool and cut into bars. Makes 36 to 48 bars.

Larry's Luscious Fudge

⅔ cup cocoa
3 cups sugar
Pinch of salt
1½ cups milk
¼ cup butter
1 teaspoon vanilla

Mix cocoa, sugar and salt in a saucepan; gradually add milk. Cook on medium heat until the hard-ball stage. Remove from heat; add butter and vanilla. Beat with wooden spoon to make it more creamy. Pour into a well-buttered 9x13-inch pan. Add chopped pecans, if desired.

Ho, Ho Butter Crunch Toffee

1 cup butter
1 cup sugar
2 Tablespoons water
1 Tablespoon light corn syrup
¾ cup nuts, finely chopped
Four 1-ounce squares semi-sweet chocolate

Melt butter in a saucepan over low heat. Remove from heat; add sugar and return to heat; stir until it begins to bubble. Add water and corn syrup. Place candy thermometer in the pan. Cook on low heat until thermometer reaches 290 degrees or brittle stage, about 20 minutes; add nuts, stirring quickly. Pour onto a lightly-greased jellyroll pan. Pan must have sides. Spread to ¼-inch thick. Cool to room temperature. Use a spatula to loosen the candy 2 or 3 times. Melt 2 squares semi-sweet chocolate in double boiler. Spread evenly over crunch. Set aside until firm; then turn over. Melt remaining chocolate to cover other side. When firm, break in pieces. Store in a tightly-covered container. Makes 1 pound of delicious candy.

You may want to use more chocolate and spread it a little thicker. Cool in the refrigerator for faster completion. This candy is worth it!

Easy Peanut-Chocolate Candy

2 Tablespoons peanut butter
One 6-ounce package butterscotch morsels
One 6-ounce package semi-sweet chocolate morsels
2 cups salted Spanish peanuts

Combine peanut butter, butterscotch morsels and chocolate morsels in a heavy saucepan. Place over low heat and stir until melted. Stir in peanuts. Drop by rounded teaspoonfuls onto waxed paper. Chill until firm. Store in covered container in refrigerator. Makes about 4 dozen.

Make Your Own Pecan Logs

One 7½-ounce jar marshmallow creme
1 teaspoon vanilla
3½ cups confectioner's sugar
1 pound caramels
9 cups chopped nuts

Combine marshmallow creme and vanilla; add sugar. Shape into rolls about 1 inch in diameter. Wrap in plastic wrap and freeze for at least 6 hours. Melt caramels over hot water; keep warm. Dip candy rolls in caramels, then roll in nuts until well coated. Store candy in a covered container. Makes about 5 pounds.

Wow Chocolate Trifle

One 19.8-ounce package fudge brownie mix, prepared
according to directions
½ cup Kahlua
Three 3.9-ounce packages instant chocolate pudding mix, prepared
according to directions
One 12-ounce container frozen whipped topping, thawed
Six 1.4-ounce Heath bars, crushed

Prick warm baked brownies with a fork; drizzle Kahlua over; let cool and
then crumble the brownies. Place ⅓ of the crumbled brownies in the bottom of large trifle bowl; top with pudding, whipped topping and crushed
candy bars. Repeat layers. Chill overnight. Serves 16 to 18.

Traditional Eggnog Pie

1 Tablespoon unflavored gelatin
¼ cup cold water
⅓ cup sugar
2 Tablespoons cornstarch
⅛ teaspoon salt
2 cups commercial eggnog
2 teaspoons vanilla
1 teaspoon rum extract
1 cup whipping cream, whipped
One 9-inch baked pie crust

In a small bowl, dissolve gelatin in water. In a saucepan, combine sugar, cornstarch and pinch of salt; add eggnog, stirring until smooth. Bring to boil for about 2 minutes or until thickened. Stir in gelatin. Mix well; remove from heat; add vanilla, rum extract and fold into the whipped cream. Pour into pie shell. Refrigerate until firm. Serves 6 to 8.

Special Occasion Eggnog and Coffee Pie

2 envelopes unflavored gelatin
½ cup cold coffee
2 cups hot coffee
½ cup sugar
2 eggs, separated, yolks beaten and whites beaten stiff
2 teaspoons brandy
Pinch of salt
1 cup heavy cream, whipped
1 square unsweetened chocolate
One 9-inch baked pie shell

Dissolve gelatin in cold coffee. Add to hot coffee; add sugar; pour into well-beaten egg yolks. Chill until completely cool. Add brandy and salt; fold in whipped cream and egg whites; spoon into pie shell. Garnish with shaved chocolate; chill.

Let the Children Make Lollipops

2 cups sugar
⅔ cup corn syrup
½ cup water
Flavorings, peppermint extract, lemon, cinnamon, almond – your choice
Food coloring
Lollipop sticks

Using a wooden spoon, stir first 3 ingredients in saucepan over low heat until dissolved; increase heat to high; bring to boil without stirring and cook for 15 to 20 minutes until candy thermometer reaches 300 degrees. Remove from heat; blend in flavorings and coloring. Slowly pour free form shapes onto a foil-lined baking sheet. Can pour shapes of Christmas trees, Christmas wreaths, angels, stockings, etc. While still hot, use the back of a spoon to press lollipop sticks into the mixture; decorate with sprinkles or cool and pipe a little icing on lollipops.

Smoky Mountain Nut Brittle

2 cups sugar
½ cup corn syrup
¼ cup boiling water
1 cup dry roasted peanuts
1 cup pecan pieces
1 Tablespoon butter
1 teaspoon baking soda

Cook first 3 ingredients in a heavy saucepan until sugar dissolves. Cover and cook over medium heat 2 to 3 minutes to melt sugar crystals on sides of pan. Uncover; add nuts and cook stirring occasionally to hard crack stage, 300 degrees on candy thermometer. Remove from heat; stir in butter and soda. Pour into a buttered 15x10-inch jellyroll pan. Spread. After brittle cools, break into pieces. Makes 1½ pounds.

Gift Giving Goodies

Gift of Kahlua

4 cups water, divided
1¾ cups sugar
1 cup cold water
6 Tablespoons instant coffee
1 vanilla bean
1 fifth vodka

Boil together 3 cups of water and sugar for 20 minutes; reduce heat and simmer another 15 to 20 minutes. Add 1 cup of cold water and instant coffee. In half-gallon container place vanilla bean and vodka; add cooked syrup. Seal container and place in dark place for 2 weeks. Remove vanilla bean and pour into smaller sealable containers for giving.

Cranberry Chutney

1 jalapeño pepper
3 medium green tomatoes, chopped
1 large pear, chopped
1 yellow apple, chopped
One 16-ounce can whole cranberry sauce
1 Tablespoon lime juice

Bake jalapeño pepper at 400 degrees for 20 minutes; remove seeds and chop. Cook jalapeño and next 3 ingredients on medium heat for about 5 minutes; add cranberry sauce; cook another 5 minutes; add lime juice. Serve with fish, meat or poultry. Makes 2 cups.

Baked Banana Bread to Share

1 stick butter
1 cup sugar
2 eggs
3 ripe bananas, mashed
2 cups flour
1 teaspoon baking soda
½ cup chopped pecans
Dash of salt

Cream butter, sugar and eggs; add bananas; stir in mixture of flour and soda; add nuts and salt. Bake in a greased loaf pan at 350 degrees for 45 to 60 minutes. Wrap in pretty foil or decorative plastic wrap. Makes 1 loaf.

Nut Bread for Friends

¾ cup sugar
2 Tablespoons shortening
1 egg
1½ cups milk
3 cups flour
3½ teaspoons baking powder
1 teaspoon salt
¾ cup chopped nuts

Mix sugar, shortening and egg; stir in milk. Sift together dry ingredients; add to liquid mixture; add nuts. Pour into a greased 9x5-inch loaf pan. Bake 60 to 70 minutes at 350 degrees. Cool thoroughly before slicing. Great for special sandwiches or with cream cheese.

Welcome Home Apple Bread

1 cup vegetable oil
3 eggs
2 cups sugar
1 teaspoon vanilla
3 cups flour
1 teaspoon cinnamon
1 teaspoon baking soda
½ teaspoon salt
3 cups diced apples
1 cup walnuts

Mix together oil, eggs, sugar and vanilla. In separate bowl blend flour, cinnamon, soda and salt; add to oil mixture; add apples and nuts to mixture. Pour batter into 2 large loaf pans. Bake at 300 degrees for 1½ hours. Cool 10 minutes before removing from pans. Wrap in foil. Makes 2 loaves.

Betty's Party Mix

6 Tablespoons butter
2 Tablespoons Worcestershire sauce
2 teaspoons seasoned salt
1 teaspoon garlic powder
½ to 2 teaspoons ground, hot red pepper
2 cups Corn Chex
2 cups Rice Chex
2 cups Wheat Chex
2 cups Honey Nut Cheerios
2 cups Bugles
1 cup potato sticks
1 pound can mixed nuts or 2 cups pecans
1 cup pretzels

Melt butter in a large 9x13-inch pan. Stir in seasonings. Add remaining ingredients. Stir until all has been coated. Bake 1 hour at 250 degrees, stirring every 15 minutes. Makes about 12 cups mix. Store in an airtight container or divide into smaller gift containers.

Gift Giving Pralines

2 cups sugar
1 teaspoon soda
1 cup buttermilk
Dash of salt
2 Tablespoons butter
1 Tablespoon light corn syrup
2½ cups pecan halves

Combine sugar, soda, buttermilk and salt in heavy saucepan; cook over medium heat to 210 degrees on a candy thermometer. Stirring constantly, add butter, syrup and pecans; continue cooking until the thermometer reaches 234 (soft ball stage). Remove from heat, beat with wooden spoon for 2 or 3 minutes until mixture begins to thicken. Drop by tablespoonfuls onto lightly-buttered waxed paper. Let cool. Wrap in colored paper and place in decorative airtight tins. Makes 18 to 24 pralines.

Tree Trimming Party Candy

One 16-ounce package white chocolate bark
½ cup crushed peppermint candy

In a heavy saucepan melt white chocolate bark, stirring with a wooden spoon. After candy melts, add crushed peppermint; stir. Pour into a foil-lined jellyroll pan. After it cools at room temperature or in the refrigerator, break into candy-size pieces. Other flavorings can be substituted for the peppermint. Package for giving.

Dipped Treats

4 to 5 medium apples
4 to 5 wooden Popsicle sticks
One 14-ounce package caramels
2 Tablespoons water
1½ cups chopped walnuts or pecans
Two 4-ounce packages sweet chocolate
2 teaspoons butter

Wash and dry apples, insert sticks. Microwave caramels and water in small deep microwave bowl on high 2 to 3 minutes until caramels are melted. Stir every minute.

Dip apples in hot caramel mixture; turn until well coated. Roll bottom half in nuts. Place on greased tray. Refrigerate at least 15 minutes. Microwave chocolate and butter in deep microwave bowl on high 2 to 3 minutes; stir until chocolate is melted. Drizzle apples with chocolate. Let stand until chocolate is firm. May substitute 20 pretzel logs for the apples.

188   MERRY CHRISTMAS

Index